Building Tax Culture, Compliance and Citizenship

A GLOBAL SOURCE BOOK
ON TAXPAYER EDUCATION

OECD
BETTER POLICIES FOR BETTER LIVES

FIIAPP
COOPERACIÓN ESPAÑOLA

EUROsociAL
PROGRAMA PARA LA COHESIÓN SOCIAL EN AMÉRICA LATINA

This work is published under the responsibility of the Secretary-General of the OECD. The opinions expressed and arguments employed herein do not necessarily reflect the official views of OECD member countries, the International and Ibero-American Foundation for Administration and Public Policies or the European Union.

This document and any map included herein are without prejudice to the status of or sovereignty over any territory, to the delimitation of international frontiers and boundaries and to the name of any territory, city or area.

Please cite this publication as:
OECD/The International and Ibero-American Foundation for Administration and Public Policies (FIIAPP) (2015), *Building Tax Culture, Compliance and Citizenship: A Global Source Book on Taxpayer Education*, OECD Publishing, Paris.
http://dx.doi.org/10.1787/9789264205154-en

ISBN 978-92-64-22335-6 (print)
ISBN 978-92-64-20515-4 (PDF)

The statistical data for Israel are supplied by and under the responsibility of the relevant Israeli authorities. The use of such data by the OECD is without prejudice to the status of the Golan Heights, East Jerusalem and Israeli settlements in the West Bank under the terms of international law.

Photo credits: Cover © designaart-Fotolia.com.

Corrigenda to OECD publications may be found on line at: *www.oecd.org/about/publishing/corrigenda.htm*.

Foreword

Taxpayer education is rapidly becoming a strategic business line of tax administrations. As governments and their tax administrations the world over are exploring alternative approaches to complement traditional enforcement-based techniques, they turn to taxpayer education programmes to improve tax compliance and tax morale.

In parallel, tax administrations have gradually undergone a transformation from being tax collection agencies to becoming service providers for citizens, positioning themselves as the bridge between the state and the citizens. This reflects the growing awareness that tax collection can also enhance accountability between citizens and the state, in addition to raising the revenue needed to fund essential services.

Building Tax Culture, Compliance and Citizenship: A Global Source Book on Taxpayer Education captures this change of approach through a sample of innovative ideas for taxpayer education from Asia, the Baltic region, the Caribbean, Latin America, the Middle East, North Africa and sub-Saharan Africa. It focuses on activities for citizens conducted by national tax administrations as well as on the issues of how and why taxes have to be paid, with strong links to the social expenditure aspect of the public finance equation.

This report is a key output of the OECD's Task Force on Tax and Development, which was created in 2010 to reflect the importance of strengthening domestic resource mobilisation as a means for countries to define their own development agenda. The Task Force advises the OECD on how to improve the enabling environment for developing countries to collect taxes fairly and effectively.

We hope this report can further contribute to the emerging global discussion and literature on the importance of taxpayer education and its role in modern tax collection strategies. We would like to stress the significance of development co-operation in supporting tax systems in developing countries. We hope this source book will serve as a guide to development practitioners on how to include taxpayer education modules in their future development co-operation programmes and that it can be an inspiration for the development of strategies, outreach and literacy campaigns.

Acknowledgements

This *Source Book on Taxpayer Education* was commissioned by the OECD's Task Force on Tax and Development and is the product of a partnership between the OECD and EUROsociAL II, the European Union's regional programme for social cohesion in Latin America led by the International and Ibero-American Foundation for Administration and Public Policies (FIIAPP). It was produced and co-ordinated by Keith Patterson, Policy Advisor of Tax and Development (OECD), with guidance from Ben Dickinson, Head of Tax and Development (OECD) and in close collaboration with Borja Díaz Rivillas, Senior Public Finance and Good Governance Officer (FIIAP) who co-ordinated and edited the chapters for the Latin American countries and contributed to the overview chapter. Special thanks are due to Marc Berenson, of the Institute of Development Studies, who conceived much of the content of the book.

This book would not have been possible without the essential contributions of the dedicated, hard-working officials in 28 tax administrations the world over, whose responsibility is to convince their fellow citizens that paying their taxes is important for them as individuals and for the good of their country, and to demonstrate to them that it is becoming ever easier to do so given new technologies. In some cases they must also convince their own senior management that taxpayer education is in the long-term strategic interest of the tax administration itself. These men and women provided essential inputs for this publication by taking the time to fill in surveys and templates and answer questions.

We would like to thank in particular: in Bangladesh, Khan Meftha Uddin, Director General, Bangladesh Civil Service (BCS); in Bhutan, the Tax Academy and Ugyen Wangdi, Deputy Collector, Department of Revenue & Customs, Tax Administration Division at the Ministry of Finance; in Brazil, Antônio Henrique Lindemberg Baltazar, Tax Auditor, Co-ordinator of Tax Education, Secretariat of the Federal Revenue of Brazil, Clóvis Belbute Peres, Tax Auditor, Secretariat of the Federal Revenue of Brazil and João Maurício Vital, Tax Auditor, Co-ordinator-General of Taxpayer Service and Tax Education, Secretariat of the Federal Revenue of Brazil; in Burundi, Domitille Mukandori, Director of Taxpayer Communication and Services, Burundi Revenue Authority (OBR); in Chile, Jorge Guzman, Head of the Internal Tax Service Education Programme; in Colombia, Francisco Ruiz Peronard, Adviser to the General Director of the National Directorate of Taxes and Custom (DIAN); in Costa Rica, Billie Brenes, Director of Taxpayer Services of the General Directorate of Taxation and Daniela Chacón, Sub-Director for Tax Education and Culture of the General Directorate of Taxation; in Egypt, Wagdy Abdelkader, Technical Office for the Egyptian Minister of Finance; in El Salvador, Evelyn Carballo, Head of the Tax Education Department, El Salvador General Directorate of Internal Taxes; the Estonian Tax and Customs Board; in Guatemala, Sergio Estrada, Consultant, Tax Culture Education Programme, Superintendence for Tax Administration (SAT); in Jamaica, Meris Haughton, Director of Communications, Tax Administration Jamaica; in Kenya, Ezekiel Maru, Deputy Commissioner, Kenya Revenue Authority; in Korea, the Korean National

Tax Service; in Lebanon, Thérèse Ghossein, Director, Bureau du civisme fiscal, ministère des Finances; in Malaysia, the Inland Revenue Service of Malaysia; in Mauritius, Naimduth Bissessur, Director, Mauritius Revenue Authority; in Mexico, Carlos Malpica, Head of the National Tax Education Programme, Tax Administration Service (SAT); in Morocco, Laila Alami Ouehhab, Head of Bureau, General Directorate of Taxes; in Mozambique, Susana Raimundo, Director of Image and Communication Office, and Hermínio Sueia, Director-General for Internal Control Office, Mozambique Revenue Authority; in Nigeria, Emmanuel Obeta, Director, Communication and Liaison, Federal Inland Revenue Service; in Peru, Carmen Vargas, Co-ordinator of the Tax Culture Programme SUNAT, Institution of Tax and Customs Administration of Peru; in Rwanda, Dorcella Mukashyaka, Director for Taxpayer Services, Rwanda Revenue Authority; in Senegal, Ange Mancabou, Director, Bureau de la communication et des relations avec le public, Direction générale des impôts et des domaines; in Singapore, the Inland Revenue Authority of Singapore; in South Africa, Jabulile Khumalo, Sobantu Ndlangalavu, Collen Lediga, all from the South African Revenue Service; in Turkey, the Turkish Revenue Administration; in Uruguay, Margarita Faral, Deputy Advisor, General Directorate of Taxation (DGI); and in Zambia, Bridget Chepeshi, Advice and Call Centre Manager, Zambia Revenue Authority.

Thanks is also given to those representatives of other countries who participated in the early stages of our information gathering but which are not reflected in this version of the source book.

We would also like to thank several contributors for providing inputs to this report, including Emma Barr and Maria Kuss of the Institute of Development Studies, Devi Thani of the Forum on Tax Administration Secretariat (OECD), Dr. Attiya Waris of the University of Nairobi and Mohammed Hameed Khudhair Al-Darkazali of the University of Sussex. Fiona Hinchcliffe provided invaluable editorial assistance and Jennifer Allain typeset and contributed to graphic design.

Table of contents

Tables

Figure

Executive summary

Governments in the developing world are striving more than ever to mobilise greater tax revenues. In light of the global recession and shrinking development funds, a country's own resources are needed in order to achieve sustainable development, relieve poverty, reduce inequalities, deliver public services and build the infrastructure for inclusive growth.

One promising way to support domestic resource mobilisation is to foster an overall culture of tax compliance that is based on rights and responsibilities, and in which citizens see paying taxes as an integral part of their relationship with the government. Across the globe, governments and tax administrations are thus developing innovative taxpayer education programmes to inform and engage both current and future taxpayers.

Preparing the next generation by creating tax-literate schoolchildren and university students is an important objective of taxpayer education programmes. This can begin with schoolchildren of primary and secondary level, which are at a key moment in their socialisation and tax awareness process. Ensuring the continuity of taxpayer education until university level also provides important opportunities to educate young adults in tax matters as part of their transition to the job market.

Taxpayer education is not only a strategy for collecting more revenue, nor is it exclusively focused on explaining why taxes should be paid. Rather, it attempts to strengthen attitudes of commitment to the common good by emphasising the social value of tax and its link to public expenditure. It highlights how public money is spent and emphasises the detrimental effects of tax fraud and corruption for a country and its citizens. Tax compliance is thereby connected to citizenship and collective responsibility.

This objective requires taxpayer education programmes to focus on a variety of educational themes. These include raising public awareness of new tax laws and methods of filing, answering public inquiries, making life easier for taxpayers or explaining the downsides of the informal sector where taxes may not be paid.

While the 28 country cases in this book suggest the optimal mode of delivering taxpayer education programmes is still an open question, new information and communication technologies offer a wide array of approaches to reach the target audiences and optimise limited resources through their multiplier effect. With theatre, video games, television shows and interactive play spaces, taxpayer education can also be a truly entertaining experience. Other opportunities include focusing on celebrating annual tax days or organising festivals around taxes. Peer learning and exchange of knowledge through regional tax organisations play an important role in distilling and promoting good practices.

Taken together, the country cases show that successful taxpayer education programmes rest on partnerships, backed by high-level political commitment. Sound partnerships, be they domestic, regional or international, can ensure sustainability and support long-term cultural change. For programmes targeting schoolchildren or university students, it is crucial to build solid alliances with the country's education sector, usually the Ministry of Education. Other key partners include business and civil society, as well as well-known public figures, such as singers, actors or sport stars, which can also play an active role for taxpayer education initiatives.

Measuring the impact of taxpayer education programmes is still a fairly new process, especially in Latin America and Africa, requiring further work and research on the impact of taxpayer education on improved tax compliance and strengthening the relationship between citizens and governments. Through peer learning our knowledge base could be expanded to issues such as ways to reach out to the informal sector, making optimal use of new technologies, the role of business and civil society, and the process of behavioural change that spans generations.

Development co-operation could play a more prominent role in supporting tax administrations and governments overcoming the main constraints to conducting their taxpayer education programmes. These constraints are related to the limited availability of time, finance and human resources. Evaluating, measuring and determining the causality of any change in taxpayer behaviour is challenging in itself, making it even more difficult to set as a political priority or strategic goal. For these reasons, development co-operation should focus on incorporating initiatives on taxpayer education in donor-funded tax or public financial management programmes.

Examples of promising development co-operation in this area include the work of the European Union through the EUROsociAL programme in El Salvador and Costa Rica, support provided by the German Development Co-operation (GIZ) agency in several countries (e.g. in Zambia) as well as bilateral initiatives such as USAID and TradeMark East Africa in Burundi, Denmark's DANIDA in Bhutan and the United Nations Development Programme (UNDP) in Lebanon.

Chapter 1

Overview: A new era for taxpayer education

This chapter first introduces the concept of taxpayer education and how it can strengthen tax compliance and the state-citizen relationship. The second part summarises the wide range of ways that national tax administrations of developing countries use to explain how and why taxes should be paid. Finally, the chapter highlights the obstacles and challenges that taxpayer education programmes face and concludes with some avenues for future discussion.

Many developing countries are at a critical stage on their path towards sustainable development, struggling to relieve poverty, reduce inequalities, deliver public services and build the infrastructure for inclusive growth. For many, the global recession has slowed the pace of growth, reducing the availability of funds for development. In this new environment, governments are striving more than ever to mobilise greater tax revenue domestically. To do so, they are increasingly reaching out to inform and engage today's – and future – taxpayers. The goal is to foster an overall "culture of compliance" based on rights and responsibilities, in which citizens see paying taxes as an integral aspect of their relationship with their government. In this context, taxpayer education becomes the bridge linking tax administration and citizen.

All over the world, innovative techniques are springing up for building this culture of compliance. This volume brings together ideas from Latin America and the Caribbean, sub-Saharan Africa, Asia, North Africa and the Middle East, and the Baltic. Most, but not all, come from developing and emerging countries. The result is a source book for developing countries, containing a wealth of ideas on how to engage taxpayers in interesting and practical ways that can be adapted to different contexts.

This source book has been put together by the OECD and EUROsociAL (the European Union's regional programme for social cohesion in Latin America), in collaboration with the Institute of Development Studies (IDS), the Forum on Tax Administration (FTA) and 28 tax administrations around the world.

What is taxpayer education and how can it help?

Taxpayer education covers a wide range of activities and actors – from government programmes to encourage tax-compliant behaviour, to efforts by business organisations to mobilise and represent the interests of their members on tax issues, to civil society initiatives to bring citizens into policy debates on tax collection and redistribution. This source book concentrates on the efforts of national tax administrations to show citizens how to pay their taxes and why taxes should be paid, with strong links to the social expenditure side of the public finance equation.

Recent studies, including by the OECD, indicate a link between tax morale – citizens' perceptions of tax issues – and perceptions of the quality of social expenditures. In other words, people who receive good quality public services are more willing to pay their taxes (OECD/ECLAC, 2011). Low tax morale not only weakens citizens' commitment to the common social project, it also reinforces a vicious cycle: people justify not paying their taxes on the grounds that the state is not keeping its side of the social bargain; this leads to insufficient revenue for improving services, services decline and so the cycle is perpetuated.

Tax evasion is a complex phenomenon reflecting a low fear of punishment; limited enforcement; and a lack of awareness of, or confidence that, the state collects taxes in a fair and efficient manner or uses the revenue to benefit most citizens. Related factors such as corruption also contribute. Despite efforts to create specialised agencies to fight corruption, to increase transparency and access to public information, corruption continues to erode trust in public institutions, limiting the potential for development.

This low satisfaction with public services and with the functioning of democracy and key state institutions – including tax authorities – can weaken civic culture and undermine tax compliance. Latin Americans, for example, perceive that half their fellow citizens do not duly pay their taxes and only 47% consider tax payment as an essential aspect of citizenship (Latinobarómetro, 2010). On average, 34% of Latin Americans define tax evasion as "never justifiable", as opposed to 62% of citizens in OECD economies; 20% justify tax evasion as opposed to 7% in OECD countries (OECD, 2012).

The large informal economy in most developing countries is another important reason for engaging in taxpayer education. A simple cost-benefit analysis is likely to show that chasing many potential taxpayers whose contribution would likely be minimal drains more resources than it brings in. However, engaging and educating them can help to strengthen feelings of responsibility and identity to the state.

Increasing numbers of governments and their tax administrations recognise these challenges and are addressing them. We are witnessing a transformation in state-citizen relations and a cultural shift in tax administrations themselves. Tax administrations are turning to positive messages to inform taxpayers of their responsibilities. Many are helping them use new technologies and are launching new services to make it easier for taxpayers to comply. The massive scope of modern tax systems necessitates a new communication model that convinces taxpayers, rather than forcing them, to pay taxes. Citizens are seen more and more as allies than mere obligation holders. These efforts are especially relevant in those countries where tax administrations were historically perceived as coercive and repressive agents. However, while tax administrations may have changed, public perceptions may take some time to catch up.

This new scenario has smoothed the way for tax administrations to take one step further: to connect tax compliance to citizenship and the values upholding collective responsibility and democratic co-existence. Taxpayer education in essence is not simply a strategy to collect more money, nor is it exclusively focused on explaining why tax should be paid. Rather, it tries to foster attitudes of commitment to the common good, emphasising the social value of tax and its link to public expenditures. This includes highlighting how public money is used and the detrimental effects of tax fraud and corruption for the country and its citizens. Research – including the OECD/ITC study, *Tax and Development: Aid Modalities for Strengthening Tax Systems* (OECD, 2013) – notes that such taxpayer education campaigns can be an efficient and effective way of building trust and increasing public engagement.

Tax authorities are aware that it is very difficult to shift tax culture without education at an early age or without citizens voluntarily embracing tax payment. A state's failure to socialise ethical values based on justice, solidarity and the "common good" can limit compliance. The investments being made in school-based and children's activities reflect the efforts of tax administrations to bring about a long-term cultural shift in attitudes and behaviour towards taxes. The idea of citizenship, based on rights and responsibilities, is a key element of many taxpayer education programmes. Active participation in one's society, through tax and broader discussion, is essential in this new citizenship construction process.

These efforts are, for the most part, fairly new. Most taxpayer education programmes, especially in Latin America and Africa, were created over the last decade. Yet despite this short history, taxpayer education is increasingly being included amongst the strategic business lines of tax administrations.

A range of themes

This source book reflects a range of educational themes: teaching taxpayers how to file their taxes; keeping them informed of changes in tax laws; encouraging people to pay their taxes; and building tax-literate schoolchildren and university students.

Raising awareness and making life easier

Countries have developed a myriad of ways to raise the public's awareness of new tax laws and methods of filing, to answer the public's inquiries and to make life easier for taxpayers. Lebanon has established a unique desktop tax calendar to remind value-added tax (VAT) taxpayers of filing dates (Chapter 15). Korea holds classes for individuals and small businesses to explain how the tax system works (Chapter 14). Singapore's new No-Filing Service is more efficient for taxpayers and the administration alike and has increased compliance (Chapter 25). Meanwhile, recognising that it cannot be taken for granted that taxpayers know how to comply, South Africa has created a stronger presence in rural areas through mobile vehicles that bring tax information to the people (Chapter 26). Zambia's weekly radio programme, Tax Chat, allows taxpayers to call in live and ask questions (Chapter 29).

Tackling the informal sector

While there is no universally accepted definition or measure of the informal sector, it is the norm in low- and most middle-income countries, estimated to account for nearly two-thirds of the global working population (even more in developing countries) (OECD, 2009). Broadening the tax base to reduce informality and non-payment of tax is a primary or secondary target of many of the initiatives described in this report. Several countries are making intensive efforts to persuade small traders to register for VAT on the one hand, whilst also encouraging consumers – through lotteries, children's games, etc. – to get into the habit of asking for official receipts when shopping. This approach has seen teams of trained students in Burundi working with small traders in shopping centres to help them enter the tax net by registering for a taxpayer identification number (TIN) (Chapter 5). Turkey has run a nationwide multi-media marketing campaign to show taxpayers and potential taxpayers how to use the new pre-filled e-tax return for rental income, which was largely being under-reported (Chapter 27).

Reaching the next generation

At school…

Work with schoolchildren (both primary and secondary) is a recurring theme in many of these examples. This segment of the population is at a key moment in its socialisation and tax awareness process. By reaching young people, tax administrations aim to bring about a long-term cultural shift. For example, in 2012, Jamaica expanded and re-launched its Schools Tax Education Programme (STEP), targeting not just secondary and tertiary schools, but also the primary level, through fun and engaging programmes for children (Chapter 12). Kenya implemented its Schools Outreach Programme in the same year to inculcate a taxpaying culture among future taxpayers (Chapter 13). Mauritius' tax administration has likewise undertaken tax sensitisation in secondary schools (Chapter 17). Morocco has been engaged in educating school children in tax literacy since 2000 (Chapter 19). Similarly, Malaysia targets school-aged children with its tax camp, speech competition and new Kidzania® junior tax office (Chapter 16). And, in addition to its education activities for schoolchildren, Peru began new courses in 2009 directed at primary and secondary school teachers to ensure quality teaching of tax matters (Chapter 22).

...and in university

Some taxpayer education programmes have started to work with technical college students and are beginning to reach university alumni. The university stage is an essential time to educate young people in tax matters as part of their transition to the job market. Through the Accounting and Tax Support Centres initiative in Brazil, *Receita Federal* trains university students in tax issues in order for the trainees to provide free support to low-income taxpayers and micro-entrepreneurs (Chapter 4). Mexico's Tax Administration Service (SAT) has signed an agreement with the *Universidad Nacional Autónoma de México* to teach tax culture as part of its "Tax Training and Information" subject (Chapter 18). And El Salvador has established a Tax Education Diploma aimed at changing and improving the tax culture of technical mid-level college teachers (Chapter 9).

Of course, taxpayer education programmes encompass tax citizenship publicity campaigns to educate the public at large as well. Mozambique launched its "Together We Make Mozambique" campaign in 2010, with the objective of ensuring that all citizens become familiar with tax matters. The focus is on compliance with taxpayer obligations and taxpayer rights, as well as reviving a tax-paying culture; the emphasis is on the informal sector (Chapter 20). Meanwhile, Rwanda has set up tax advisory councils to educate citizens on their role in the fight against corruption and smuggling and the role taxes play in development (Chapter 23). Bhutan's Bookkeeping Workshop for Small and Micro Businesses was also open to members of the public. It sought to remedy a recognised need to educate the public on how to keep adequate bookkeeping accounts as a precursor to paying taxes (Chapter 3).

A diversity of approaches

Tax in cyberspace

New technologies are generating many opportunities to reach the target audience and to optimise resources. The multiplier effect is clear in initiatives such as El Salvador's On-Line Tax Education Diploma (Chapter 9), Chile's SIIEduca and PlanetaSII web portals for students and educators (Chapter 6) and Uruguay's Plan Ceibal to provide every child with a laptop loaded with tax-related activities (Chapter 28). They also help to close the digital gap and smooth inequalities in access to information. New technologies require new training: Colombia has launched an information campaign to show taxpayers how to use a digital signature system for their online tax declaration (Chapter 7). Estonia educates its taxpayers on how to pay their taxes through its new e-tax/e-customs electronic service environment (Chapter 10).

Tax at the games room and on TV

Taxpayer education can be entertaining: this source book features some fun examples of how tax can be explained through interactive play spaces, theatre, video games and soap operas on television. Costa Rica has created a "Tribute to My Country" space for children at the *Museo de los Niños de San José*, a former penitentiary (Chapter 8).

Children learn about taxes and public expenditure by completing their first income tax statement, deciding how to use public funds in a mock National Assembly, pretending to be customs agents or following the path of state funds. Most countries run periodic television advertisements during tax season or after a national budget and some have introduced children's cartoon series such as Chile's *Ivo the Chinchilla* (Chapter 6). Malaysia sponsors a sitcom aimed at small and medium-sized enterprises. Nigeria has taken things further with a television soap opera – "Binding Duty" – that provides a relaxed, enjoyable and non-confrontational way of reminding citizens of their responsibility to pay taxes (Chapter 21).

Celebrating tax: Tax days and festivals

Bangladesh celebrates National Income Tax Day every year on 15 September in the run up to the formal submission day of 30 September, when more than 80% of tax returns are filed (Chapter 2). Guatemala's annual citizen culture festival "Strength Lies in Numbers" uses musical events, talent shows, plays and stands to inform citizens of the social significance of taxes (Chapter 11). Likewise, Rwanda's Taxpayer's Day serves to strengthen links between taxation and national development, promote tax compliance and build trust in the Rwanda Revenue Authority. As guest of honour, the Rwandan President gives awards to the country's best taxpayers (Chapter 23). Senegal launched annual National Information Days in 2008 to tackle citizens' lack of knowledge of tax regulations and unwillingness to comply with tax administration officials (Chapter 24). The Information Days provided a key platform for informing and engaging Senegalese on new tax reforms.

What are the keys to success?

Solid partnerships

Comparative experience demonstrates that for taxpayer education programmes to have a lasting impact they must work through partnerships – domestically, regionally and even internationally.

Achieving the long-term, sustainable cultural change envisioned by taxpayer education champions requires building solid alliances with the education sector, making this a critical challenge for taxpayer education. Working with ministries of education is key for enabling tax authorities to engage with schools and to develop content that is relevant and accessible to students – the next generation of potential taxpayers. Formal agreements can be reached with education ministries and institutions to guide joint discussions on approach, content and challenges. Although building solid partnerships between ministries can be a long and difficult process, the experiences here are cause for optimism. Several ministries of education are beginning to see the benefits of collaborating with tax authorities: such collaboration can enrich the curricula on social studies, accounting or tax. In Latin America alone, nine countries have included tax education in their school syllabi and have developed material jointly with ministries of education. For examples see the chapters from El Salvador (Chapter 9) and Peru (Chapter 22) in this source book, and also EUROsociAL's work in Latin America.[1]

Other useful partners can be business and civil society. Jamaica worked with a non-governmental organisation that promotes entrepreneurship (Junior Achievement) to help deliver its educational programme for business students. Singapore engages businesses through its Taxpayer Feedback Panel and promotes volunteerism in the community through the nationwide Volunteer e-Filing Service. Rwanda created its Tax Issue Forum with the Private Sector Federation and the business community in mind. Brazil trains students to support low-income and other vulnerable groups with tax matters.

Tax champions

High-level political commitment and participation are other key elements of many initiatives. In Rwanda, the President himself gives out annual taxpayer awards, while Turkey's Minister of Finance spoke directly to taxpayers on YouTube. Senior national and local politicians lead taxpayer education events in many countries, including the Minister of the Economy and Finance of Senegal and the Mayor of Quetzaltenango in Guatemala. In March 2013, Costa Rica's President and the Ministers of Education and Finance decreed tax education a public interest matter, and made a national commitment to promote tax culture.

Other well-known figures can also help convey messages to a potentially sceptical audience. For its National Income Tax Day, Bangladesh, for instance, brought on board popular singers and actors as well as cricket and football players. Turkey attracted a popular national comedian to support its campaign on pre-filled rental income tax returns.

Cross-country learning

Regional organisations can act as knowledge exchange fora on taxpayer education. The Inter-American Center of Tax Administrations (CIAT) has brought its members together to discuss tax morale, taxpayer education and related issues, posting useful documentation on its website. Jamaica was invited to present its STEP programme to the Caribbean Organisation of Tax Administrators (COTA). The recently incorporated African Tax Administration Forum (ATAF) held a technical seminar on taxpayer services in August 2013 in Swaziland with a focus on taxpayer orientation and communication. The Intra-European Organisation of Tax Administrations (IOTA) held a workshop in October 2013 on "Improving Compliance by Education" in the Former Yugoslav Republic of Macedonia, building on its 2008 workshop on "Fiscal Education of the Young".

A role for development co-operation?

Taxpayer education is an oft-overlooked area of development co-operation. The European Union, through its EUROsociAL programme, has been undertaking important work in this area. EUROsociAL works with tax administrations and education ministries across Latin America to build capacity and exchange knowledge on taxpayer education through the lens of social cohesion. For example, it helped to arrange for Argentina to share its experience and expertise on creating tax-themed children's play areas with El Salvador (also sponsored by USAID) and Costa Rica (see Chapters 8 and 9). The German Development Co-operation (GIZ) agency supports taxpayer education in several countries. GIZ support for Zambia's new Taxpayer Education Unit included funding a study tour for Zambian tax officials to Nepal in 2013 (Chapter 29). Bilateral initiatives include USAID and TradeMark East Africa in Burundi (Chapter 5), Denmark's DANIDA in Bhutan (Chapter 3) and the United Nations Development Programme (UNDP) in Lebanon (Chapter 15).

Obstacles and challenges

Taxpayer education faces the usual obstacles of limited time, financial and human resources. When making the hard choices about allocating scarce resources, some far-sighted tax administrations have embraced taxpayer education as a strategic objective, while others leave it to dedicated officials to fit this important work around their main jobs. Making the case for taxpayer education to be seen as a priority can be particularly difficult given the challenges with evaluating, measuring and determining the causality of any change in taxpayer behaviour.

Other challenges include getting the tax policy framework right. The Bhutan case study illustrates how policy adjustments can enhance the effectiveness of tax education: in this case by requiring small traders to conduct minimal bookkeeping. Chile has found that new technologies bring new burdens: keeping websites up to speed with rapidly changing navigation and content needs. Colombia sought to tackle the lack of a "computer culture" among citizens head on, while El Salvador dealt with fear of technological tools for training by placing one of the first lessons of its Tax Education Diploma programme online. Meanwhile, Morocco fought the high cost of audiovisual broadcasts by obtaining free or substantially discounted broadcasts of television spots and radio messages. And, then, as noted by Mauritius, perhaps, the most important lesson of all for any taxpayer education activity: if the tax administration had not undertaken this initiative – a tax literacy campaign for the benefit of future taxpayers in this case – no one else would have.

Continuing the conversation

This volume is a contribution to the emerging global conversation on the importance of taxpayer education, the role it plays in improving compliance and strengthening the relationship between citizens and government, and how to go about it. Looking ahead, there is potential to go further in several areas:

- Exchange knowledge and share best practices on themes such as those seen in this volume: outreach to the informal sector; school-based and children's programmes; the use of new technologies to make the tax assessment experience of taxpayers much easier and to educate them about it (as in Colombia, Estonia, Malaysia, Singapore and Turkey); and the roles of business and civil society in taxpayer education. Morocco's strategy for educating the diaspora and Korea's use of its embassies to reach Koreans living abroad may be of wider interest. Fragile countries could learn from the experiences of post-conflict ones such as Burundi and Rwanda, and Rwanda itself – which has also embraced the "one laptop per child" initiative – could learn from Uruguay's efforts to turn this into a platform to raise awareness of tax issues amongst future taxpayers while they have fun!
- Measure the impact of taxpayer education initiatives in terms of enhanced compliance (numbers/percentage of taxpayers; revenue) and improved tax morale. Measuring behavioural change, particularly when looking over the span of a generation, is not easy for any tax administration. Some efforts have been made (see, for example, Chapter 26 on South Africa and Chapter 29 on Zambia), which could be shared as a foundation for future work that would benefit all countries.

- Expand regional co-operation following the Latin America and Caribbean model. EUROsociAL, CIAT, COTA and an increasing number of national tax administrations are actively working together in this region. Other regions are following suit and discussions could continue, starting perhaps with the participants in this source book.
- Focus development co-operation support: The OECD/ITC study (OECD, 2013) recommended that every donor-funded tax programme should, if possible, incorporate programmes for public information, tax education programmes and public-private dialogue. Bilateral and multilateral development agencies could look at the examples contained here and expand their efforts to support taxpayer education. There are strong links to domestic resource mobilisation and support for effective institutions. As noted in the OECD's *Draft Principles for International Engagement in Supporting Developing Countries in Revenue Matters* consideration could be given to supporting civil society organisations in their efforts to promote the participation of citizens in policy debates on tax collection and redistribution.[2]

Notes

1. See, for example, EUROsociAL/Instituto de Estudios Fiscales (2010).
2. www.oecd.org/ctp/tax-global/Principles_for_international_engagement_May2013.pdf.

References

EUROsociAL/Instituto de Estudios Fiscales (2010), *Educacion Fiscal y Cohesion Social: Experiencias de America Latina*, EUROsociAL/Instituto de Estudios Fiscales, www.eurosocialfiscal.org/uploads/documentos/centrodoc/d1cc7ba6323ad05a8e11113bed6d6814.pdf (in Spanish).

Latinobarómetro (2010), *2009 Latinobarómetro Report*, Corporación Latinobarómetro, Santiago de Chile, www.latinobarometro.org.

Nerré, B. (2008), "Tax culture: A basic concept for tax politics", *Economic Analysis & Policy*, Vol. 38, No. 1, March, available at: https://docs.google.com/file/d/18H3eX7eKiZBK6wrYVI6VqLpnFKn1JGZc_PS1lY-2sGbrWaMVS11FHeVIbBwn/edit?pli=1.

OECD (2013), *Tax and Development: Aid Modalities for Strengthening Tax Systems*, OECD Publishing, Paris, http://dx.doi.org/10.1787/9789264177581-en.

OECD (2012), "What drives tax morale?", *OECD Development Centre Working Papers*, No. 315, OECD Publishing, Paris, http://dx.doi.org/10.1787/5k8zk8m61kzq-en.

OECD (2009), *Is Informal Normal? Towards More and Better Jobs in Developing Countries*, OECD Publishing, Paris, http://dx.doi.org/10.1787/9789264059245-en.

OECD/ECLAC (2011), *Latin American Economic Outlook 2012: Transforming the State for Development*, OECD Publishing, Paris, http://dx.doi.org/10.1787/leo-2012-en.

Chapter 2

Bangladesh: National Income Tax Day

Bangladesh's National Board of Revenue (NBR)

This chapter presents Bangladesh's taxpayer education programme. It first describes the broad objectives of the programme, followed by a focus on a specific element of the programme, the National Income Tax Day. It subsequently looks at the impact and lessons learnt of the initiative, followed by next steps.

Bangladesh has a very narrow tax base and a very small percentage of the population bears the burden of taxation (less than 1%; NBR, 2011). The National Board of Revenue (NBR; see Box 2.2), Bangladesh's main tax administration body, suspects there is gross under-reporting or non-reporting and that tax performance across the board is much less than it should be, given the country's GDP and economic growth. At 9.3%, Bangladesh's tax-to-GDP ratio is also quite low when compared with other, similarly-placed countries in South Asia (NBR, 2011). In response to these challenges, the NBR has embarked on far-reaching reforms of its tax policy and tax administration. The latter seek to centralise and automate tax accounts and processing of tax returns. These are being coupled with the creation of an efficient *Taxpayer Identification Number (TIN) database* as a valuable tool for analysing taxpayer profile and behaviour. The NBR is also building strong back-end systems and data management capacity by centralising accounts, returns receipts and processing, transaction processing and taxpayer registration; and rationalising tax laws.

The analysis and information enabled by these reforms will support an aggressive taxpayer education programme to help taxpayers fulfil their duties as responsible citizens or residents and to understand how to meet their tax obligations.

Bangladesh's taxpayer education

Strategic communication is extremely important to obtain taxpayer and key stakeholder support for tax reforms. The NBR needs to strengthen its internal capacity for such communication with stakeholders, or use external firms to convey its message when necessary (Box 2.1).

Taxpayer education in Bangladesh is done by the NBR, in partnership with other government ministries and agencies, such as the Ministry of Information and other departments under the Ministry of Finance. It targets all corporate and individual taxpayers.

Box 2.1. Objectives of taxpayer education in Bangladesh

- Raise awareness of tax laws and procedures.
- Increase voluntary compliance.
- Educate tax officials to discharge their duties and responsibilities in accordance with the law, keeping in mind that they are to serve the taxpayer with utmost care and to take into account taxpayers' rights.
- Enhance the managerial capacity of tax executives.
- Show citizens how to pay taxes.
- Increase the number of citizens who pay taxes.
- Explain why taxes should be paid.
- Empower citizens to engage in discussions on the use of tax revenue.
- Increase citizens' tax literacy.

Source: Bangladesh's National Board of Revenue.

The taxpayer education programme will provide a menu of information through the Internet (the NBR has a reasonably informative and useful website) and directly through one-on-one or group contact with the NBR Customer Service Wing, which will provide direct support to taxpayers at conveniently located facilitation centres. This programme will also include setting up call centres to answer taxpayers' questions. These centres will help taxpayers prepare their returns, calculate their tax liabilities, understand tax payment deadlines and so on. The service centres will also co-ordinate taxpayer education programmes in tax offices, commerce and industry association forums, tax advocates/certified accountants forums and among community organisations.

The programme will also provide information through national television, radio and newspapers, mainly managed through the Ministry of Information; multilingual materials published by the state tax administration; seminars and workshops to raise taxpayer awareness of their rights and obligations; locating taxpayer services within other government offices to increase visibility; documentaries and dramas; billboard banners and posters; leaflets and brochures; tax fairs; and an online tax calculator to inform taxpayers of their payable tax.

Focus on: National Income Tax Day

All non-corporate taxpayers in Bangladesh must file their tax returns by 30 September. To remind citizens and registered taxpayers to pay their taxes, since 2008 the government of Bangladesh has been celebrating National Income Tax Day on 15 September.

On this day, tax departments all over the country hold street processions, seminars and workshops; display banners and posters; distribute leaflets; organise rallies and roundtable conferences; set up tax clinics along roadsides; arrange contests and awards for the highest taxpayers; and screen documentaries and dramas on taxation.

In addition to generally educating taxpayers, this celebration also aims to:

- improve taxpayer services
- inform people of relevant taxation amendments
- bridge the gap between tax officials and taxpayers
- develop a collegial atmosphere and work in co-operation with tax agents (lawyers, accountants and tax practitioners)
- eradicate corruption.

The main target groups are personal income taxpayers, corporate income taxpayers, large and medium-size firms, as well as small and micro-enterprises. Therefore, activities focus on income tax for individuals, as well as on tax on entrepreneurs and enterprise profits.

To reach as many people as possible, national, regional and local television, newspapers and radio are involved in the event. Other promotional instruments are multilingual materials published by the state tax administration, and social media such as Facebook and Twitter. Higher education institutions also are involved in the activities.

The organisation and preparation for this event starts in the last week of July and is a joint effort by the NBR along with a range of government departments and agencies, political leaders, business organisations, civil society, national popular artists (such as singers and actors) and sports icons (especially cricket and football players). It is co-ordinated by a national committee consisting of 60 members, mainly directors of divisions and key NBR personnel. There are also 7 to 10 sub-committees of around 20 members looking into different issues. Staff training and briefings for staff also take place before the event.

The initiative costs approximately BDT 30 million (USD 380 000).

Impacts

- Increase in taxes. In total, 2 to 5 million taxpayers are reached by the event every year. As a result, the number of taxpayers as well as tax revenue collected has increased substantially in recent years. Income tax collections, for example, have shown constant growth, doubling in size over the past four years. Hence, overall, the initiative is considered to be successful. There also has been a great increase in taxpayer knowledge (i.e. in the skills needed to pay taxes), as well as a great increase in people's sense of moral obligation to pay taxes "voluntarily".
- More positive perceptions. Before the initiative began, the media was rather critical of taxation and often published negative reports on the state tax administration. Since the initiative began, there has been a very large increase in the perception that taxpayers are treated fairly and transparently by the tax administration, as well as a great increase in the number of taxpayers who believe that the government spends their tax money wisely. However, this initiative is considered to have only slightly increased the perception that other taxpayers are paying their fair share.
- Improvements in tax compliance. Tax compliance over the past five years has improved greatly.

Although this initiative has not been evaluated independently, national members of parliament speak highly of the programme's success. Furthermore, an evaluation of both the lower and higher taxpayer categories indicates a discernible decrease in the number of non-filers.

Lessons learnt

This initiative has shown how important taxpayer education can be: it has enhanced citizens' tax compliance and has changed taxpayers' perceptions of the NBR. It has shown that taxpayers can be very interested in tax-related topics and that they appreciate the new client-centred approach adopted by the NBR.

The main challenge for the initiative has been compliance by tax officials and staff with the NBR's new client-centred approach. This approach requires open engagement by tax officials with clients to provide them with assistance. In the past, such direct contact was limited and so staff were reluctant to interact with the public. To change the attitudes of tax officials, discussions, brainstorming sessions and training took place. International consultants also helped to raise awareness among these officials and staff.

Another challenge has been the high costs of the initiative and the need to allocate enough money to implement the event. In the past, budget constraints have often limited the scope of the initiative.

Next steps

The NBR plans to make improvements to the event. For example, it will need to begin the various workshops and educational activities earlier in the month so as to increase support to taxpayers for filing their returns during the last weeks before the submission date.

Furthermore, more NBR personnel will need to be engaged, especially at the local level, as well as support from all political parties. This would help improve the initiative's organisation and scope.

Box 2.2. Bangladesh's National Board of Revenue (NBR)

The National Board of Revenue (NBR), established by presidential order in 1972, is Bangladesh's main tax administration body. It is located under the Internal Resources Division (IRD) of the Ministry of Finance (MoF) and is divided into three main subdivisions: the Customs Wing, VAT Wing and Income Tax Wing. It also includes IT and Research & Statistics Wings. The NBR has a staff of 8 900, divided among 649 tax offices, mostly in urban and metropolitan areas. There are 75 offices in rural areas.

Its responsibilities are to:

- collect tax revenues
- formulate and continuously re-appraise tax policies and tax laws
- negotiate tax treaties with foreign governments
- participate in inter-ministerial deliberations on economic issues having a bearing on fiscal policies and tax administration.

For more information, see: www.nbr.gov.bd.

Source: Bangladesh's National Board of Revenue.

Reference

NBR (National Board of Revenue) (2011), *Outline of Modernization Plan (2011-2016): National Board of Revenue (NBR)*, NBR, Dacca, available at: www.nbr-bd.org/tender/NBR_Modernisation_Plan_Final_draft.pdf.

Chapter 3

Bhutan: Bookkeeping workshops for small businesses

Department of Revenue and Customs (DRC)

This chapter presents Bhutan's taxpayer education programme. It first gives an overview of the whole programme and its objectives, followed by a focus on one specific element, the bookkeeping workshops for small and micro-enterprises. It subsequently looks at the impacts and lessons learnt of the initiative, followed by an outlook on next steps.

Taxpaying culture in Bhutan is a relatively new concept. The personal income tax was just introduced in 2001, for example, and just a few decades earlier (prior to 1960) tax obligations were paid "in kind", through labour contributions. The newness of certain taxes means that the Ministry of Finance's Department of Revenue and Customs (DRC; see Box 3.3) has had to start from a very low base in terms of taxpayer awareness of their obligations and how to meet them.

Taxpayer education in Bhutan

The DRC recognised the need for creative ways to educate the public on how to pay taxes, including through a personal income tax awareness campaign (Box 3.2). It soon realised that many small and micro-businesses do not keep adequate bookkeeping accounts and sought to remedy this by holding taxpayer education workshops (Box 3.1).

Box 3.1. Objectives of taxpayer education in Bhutan

- Encourage taxpayers to pay taxes.
- Increase the number of citizens who pay taxes.
- Explain the system of taxation.
- Increase the tax literacy of citizens.
- Show citizens how to pay taxes.

Source: Department of Revenue and Customs.

Staffing and funding limitations mean that the Ministry of Finance does not have a specialised division or unit for taxpayer education. However, taxpayer education is conducted by the DRC, involving all concerned divisions (Revenue and Audit, Customs and Excise, Income Tax and Sales Tax) which provide staff as and when required.

Taxpayer education activities include workshops, trainings and seminars. The DRC also has a Public Information Services Unit, responsible for dissemination of statutory public notifications through appropriate media.

Activities are aimed at all personal income taxpayers, medium-sized, small and micro-enterprises and include:

- bookkeeping seminars for small and medium enterprises
- pamphlets to guide taxpayers on how and when to file their returns, etc.
- media campaigns in national and multilingual television, newspapers and radio.

Media campaigns are mostly conducted one or two months ahead of the tax filing period so as to alert taxpayers in good time. The DRC's Public Information Services conduct media preference surveys during the tax season so as to choose the most popular media channels. One-year contracts are then drawn up with the national television and radio station (Bhutan Broadcasting Services) and the two most popular newspaper companies (most recently, Kuensel Corporation Limited and Bhutan Times Limited). At present there are 12 newspapers in the country, but some have very small circulation. Of the six radio stations, only four have coverage in the national capital. One-year contracts enable the department to get discounts of up to 40%. Initially, this arrangement was only used by the DRC; however, since it has proven to be cost effective, the broader ministry has now come on board. All advertisements are centralised and managed by the DRC's Public Information Services. With the government's commitment to enhancing nationwide broadband initiatives, the Internet will soon become a viable medium for reaching taxpayers. The DRC is also developing a real time web-based revenue administration management information system (RAMIS), aimed at providing self-service to taxpayers and to other concerned stakeholders. All 8 regional offices, 17 check-points and Paro international airport (the only international airport) will be connected to this system. This project is funded by the Asian Development Bank (ADB) and was expected to be operational by mid-2014.

The DRC was one of the first government institutions to use SMS messages through mobile telephones. However, now that many other agencies have started to use this medium, its potential has diminished somewhat.

Focus on: Bookkeeping workshops for small and micro-businesses

The DRC developed this initiative to improve business income tax compliance by small and micro-businesses. It was started in 2003 and went until 2007. In Bhutan, an estimated 80% of taxpayers fall under the small and micro-firm taxpayer category. This group is particularly challenging to tax as these businesses often do not maintain any financial records. While by law all listed corporations have to keep books of accounts, small and medium businesses are not obliged to do so. Despite being encouraged to, many do not. In the past, tax offices calculated taxes for these firms but this led to growing taxation grievances as small and micro-entrepreneurs felt that the tax office calculations were too high. This is why the DRC decided to help these taxpayers to calculate their own taxes.

Workshops and seminars were conducted to educate and encourage small and micro-businesses to maintain basic accounting records voluntarily in order to ease the tax payment process. It also intended to improve understanding of how much tax was to be paid in relation to profits, to increase tax literacy and to educate the target group in tax law. Many shopkeepers lack the educational levels required to keep accounts.

These bookkeeping workshops were simple and very basic. While not necessarily specifically focused on tax, the workshops dealt with the basic aspects of bookkeeping in relation to tax on entrepreneurs and enterprise profits tax. The workshops were conducted in a classroom format using PowerPoint presentations and handouts. The speakers were arranged by the DRC.[1]

The workshops were conducted in co-ordination with the Bhutan Chamber of Commerce and Industry, which has branch offices across the country. These offices were responsible for selecting and informing small and micro-enterprises about the workshops. In total, 15 DRC employees were involved in the bookkeeping workshop project (2 at the national level and 13 regional staff). No training was provided to staff members involved. It was the responsibility of the regional directors to implement the workshops. Workshops could be tailored to meet the requirements of a particular group.

The total cost of the project for the four-year period (2003-07) was approximately BTN 750 000 (about USD 12 000) and in all about 3 000 small and micro-businesses participated. It is important to note that from 1996 to 2007, the DRC received assistance from the Danish government through its development co-operation agency DANIDA's

Good Governance Programme. This provided technical and financial assistance for good governance. For example, a Danish tax advisor was seconded to the DRC to provide support for human resources, computers and training, in order to build capacity and broaden the tax base. In addition to the bookkeeping workshops, many other tax awareness programmes were undertaken during this period of co-operation (see Box 3.2 for another example).

Impacts

The bookkeeping workshops appear to have had limited success: there was no discernible increase in the keeping of basic accounting records for the target group in the years following the workshops. The programme has been discontinued.

An assessment by the DRC's tax assessment team in January/February 2006 found that only 2 participants out of 26 who attended a workshop in Wangdue district were maintaining basic accounting books. National follow-up assessments reveal participants' reasons for not keeping accounts despite tax officials' recommendations and demonstrations. These include the fear of unintentional consequences of keeping books, such as that keeping books would put them at risk of higher taxes being levied and that the absence of accounting books could enable them to negotiate with tax officials. The assessments also indicated that many shopkeepers do not have enough education to keep their books; some have never gone to school.

In the absence of a research unit, the best indicator of a change in taxpayer behaviour would be a rise in taxpayer numbers. In terms of bookkeeping, in the 2003 income tax year the number of business income taxpayers totalled 10 088, of which 1 008 kept accounts. In the 2010 income tax year, though the number of business income taxpayers had risen to 16 679, only 1 384 kept accounts. On the other hand, between 2003 and 2010, the total number of taxpayers in Bhutan grew by 206%: from 21 978 to 67 287. This increasing number of voluntary taxpayers could be one indication that past awareness programmes have been effective (Box 3.2), especially in the absence of any income tax "raids". It may also have been helped by a scheme in 2007, whereby the DRC gave taxpayers a two-month penalty-free window in which to declare and regularise their undeclared income.

There has been a slight increase in taxpayers' knowledge and skills for paying taxes, as well as in people's sense of moral obligation to pay taxes "voluntarily". However, the workshops seem to have done little to change the target audience's perception of the tax administration.

Box 3.2. Bhutan's awareness campaign for personal income taxpayers

Prior to the introduction of the personal income tax (PIT) in 2001, the DRC carried out a successful campaign to create awareness and educate taxpayers for a smooth introduction of the PIT. This was conducted with full support from the ministry and funding from DANIDA, the Danish government's development co-operation. The campaign concept and strategy were both designed in-house. The focus was on promoting voluntary declaration/compliance connected to nation building. At that time in Bhutan there was only one television/radio station providing daily evening and morning broadcast services; and a weekly national newspaper. Despite this, the media market was not fragmented, and most target audiences could be reached. This was further supplemented by holding workshops and setting up information booths during festival gatherings.

Lessons learnt

The fact that Bhutan's tax law does not require small and micro-enterprises to maintain financial records makes it difficult for tax inspectors to determine the amount of tax payable and to convince the taxpayer that the calculation is accurate. In such a tax policy context, measures to educate and empower taxpayers are likely to have limited impact. The programme would be more likely to succeed if there were incentives for those who decide to keep their own books, such as a reduced tax rate. The low literacy rate of the target group compounds these problems. Although the DRC continues to receive requests from the Bhutan Chamber of Commerce and Industry to continue the bookkeeping workshops for small and micro-businesses, it has stopped the initiative due to its limited impact and the lack of funding. While this initiative was of limited success even by the DRC's own criteria, it underscores the reality that for some taxpayer education initiatives to succeed, policy adjustments may be required.

Another big challenge is a shortage of staff and the low budget allocated for taxpayer education activities. The DRC needs more people and must be able to retain its cadre.

Next steps

A future target group for tax education might be non-government organisations (NGOs), which must register with the DRC to gain tax exemption. The department might have to conduct workshops with NGOs to train and educate their personal on how and why they must maintain a book of accounts even if they have been deemed tax exempt.

Box 3.3. **Bhutan's Department of Revenue and Customs (DRC)**

The Department of Revenue and Customs, which was unified into a single division in 1986, comes under the Ministry of Finance. Its mission is to ensure that the tax and customs administration has the capacity to collect taxes efficiently and effectively at minimum cost through impartial and consistent enforcement of regulations, and to provide a convenient and honest service to the taxpayers. Its vision is to contribute to the nation-building process through the development of an effective revenue system. It has a staff of 122 (divided among the Central Tax Administration and the 8 regional DRC offices, which deal directly with taxpayers). Each of the eight offices covers four or five districts. With 67 287 taxpayers in 2010, there is approximately one tax official for every 551 taxpayers.

For more information, see: www.mof.gov.bt.

Source: Department of Revenue and Customs.

Note

1. The Ministry of Economic Affairs and the Ministry of Labour and Human Resources have also organised bookkeeping workshops, sometimes jointly with the Department of Revenue and Customs.

Chapter 4

Brazil: Accounting and tax support for low-income taxpayers

Secretariat of the Federal Revenue of Brazil

This chapter presents Brazil's taxpayer education programme. It first gives an overview of the whole programme and its objectives, followed by a focus on one specific element, the university-based centres for accounting and tax support. It subsequently looks at the impact and lessons learnt of the initiative, followed by an outlook on next steps.

With over 193 million people, the Federative Republic of Brazil is the fifth largest country in the world in terms of both population and land area (8.5 million km²). A gross domestic product of USD 2 223 billion made Brazil the world's seventh wealthiest economy in 2012. That year the Secretariat of the Federal Revenue of Brazil, or *Receita Federal* as it is known in Brazil, collected over USD 500 billion in taxes.

The *Receita Federal* is an agency under the Ministry of Finance (Box 4.2). It is responsible for administering federal taxes, including collecting social security revenue, and for customs activities. The *Receita Federal* also assists the executive branch in developing tax policy, and works to prevent and combat tax evasion, contraband, smuggling, piracy, commercial fraud, drug trafficking, the trade of endangered species and other international trade-related illicit acts.

Brazil's taxpayer education

In modern populous nations like Brazil, which cover a large territory, a good tax system should combine traditional sanctions with educational mechanisms in order to promote the social acceptance of taxation. This is why the *Receita Federal* has been involved in tax education since the 1970s, when its Tax Education Programme was launched. The programme targets citizens and students, as well as civil servants, accountants and customs agents.

The central idea behind the *Receita Federal*'s Taxpayer Education Programme is to strengthen the bonds between the state and society (Box 4.1). The idea is to improve the relationship between the tax administration and the taxpayer and to disseminate knowledge on tax regulations. In turn, it increases voluntary compliance with fiscal duties, as well as the social acceptance of taxation.

Within the agency there is an understanding that tax education helps to enhance tax awareness and encourages the voluntary observation of tax rules. It also affirms to staff the importance of their work for providing a service of excellence to society as a whole. Tax education helps to improve the country's business environment by promoting discussion on tax evasion, smuggling, the informal sector and piracy. Moreover, it contributes to the macroeconomic balance, especially for public expenditures. By showing the public the reason for tax policies and how they work, it also strengthens society's image of the tax administration.

Box 4.1. Objectives of the taxpayer education programme in Brazil

- Inform citizens of their rights and duties, of the socio-economic role of taxation and of societal control of public expenditures.
- Build awareness of tax and customs obligations and make every effort to simplify them.
- Inform taxpayers of the *Receita Federal*'s services, especially its online taxpayer services.
- Contribute to continuous improvement in service quality and to integrate the agency into people's daily lives.
- Promote co-operation among institutional partners.

Source: Secretariat of the Federal Revenue of Brazil.

All of the *Receita Federal*'s units have a remit to organise tax education and are steered by published guidelines (Receita Federal, 2012). In 2012, 11 941 tax education events were held throughout the country. By June 2013, a further 4 500 events had already been organised. The various activities are co-ordinated by the General Co-ordination of Taxpayer Service and Tax Education, which is managed by the Undersecretary of Tax Collection and Taxpayer Service.

Focus on: University-based centres for accounting and tax support

By international standards, Brazil has a particularly complex tax system. This complexity affects distinct groups of citizens and professionals differently. While some citizens have access to information and can hire professional support, the economically less-favoured find it difficult to obtain tax advice through the official tax administration channels. Sometimes they also find it hard to be heard or understood at accounting offices, leading to inequality and marginalisation and preventing them from complying with their obligations. Poor people risk being marginalised by the formal tax system.

A similar challenge with complexity and unequal access was identified in the legal system; clinics have been established in the many law schools that offer legal advice to help disadvantaged people navigate the legal system. These free services allow people to benefit from the knowledge and patience of law students and from the expertise of their supervisors. This chance to offer some help creates a real-life "laboratory" for students and is a key part of their technical and social training. Such clinics have various names, but here we call them by the acronym SAJU (*Serviços de Apoio Jurídico a Pessoas Desassistidas* or Judicial Support for the Less Favoured).

The SAJU's success prompted the *Receita Federal* to support the creation of similar initiatives in accounting and overseas trade colleges whereby students help poorer people with tax matters. Although the initiative was conceived in 2008, it was not until 2011 that the first colleges accepted the challenge. Known as centres for accounting and tax support (*núcleos de apoio contábil e fiscal* or NAF), today there are 26 such centres throughout Brazil.

NAFs' objectives are:

1. to provide accounting and tax support to the economically less-favoured (such as small enterprises or people with a gross annual income of less than USD 12 000, or faculty employees who cannot afford qualified assistance)
2. to act as a centre for the generation of fiscal knowledge through discussions, visits, study groups and presentations.

The idea behind NAFs was partly inspired by the United States' experience, where non-governmental organisations (NGOs) assist poorer people with tax issues. One such American initiative are the low-income taxpayer clinics (LITC; Taxpayer Advocate Service, 2013). These are similar to NAFs, since they are not part of the tax administration and are instead run by civil society. On the other hand, NAFs are based exclusively in universities, and only use the expertise of college students. And while the LITCs limit their action to helping the disadvantaged, NAFs also participate in academic discussion on relevant tax themes and in training students to become accountants or international trade experts.

It is important to be clear about what NAFs are not:

- they are not an extension of the *Receita Federal*
- they do not replace accounting offices
- they do not represent an official contract between the *Receita Federal* and the colleges to provide tax services.

The strength of the project lies in two factors: *i)* the autonomy of the university or college as an intensive creative source; and *ii)* the institutional and technical support by the tax administration, which complements students' academic training. The advantages are clear to all participants. Citizens profit by getting help to answer the most basic tax questions. Accounting offices profit by being able to delegate certain difficult cases to NAF, including those where basic communication with the client is particularly challenging. The *Receita Federal* also profits by fulfilling its fiscal education role and by providing support to the less favoured. The university profits in at least three ways: extra development opportunities for its students; stronger bonds with the community; and a boost in its performance indicators at the Department of Education (which raises the university's profile, helps with funding, etc.).

How does NAF work?

Initially, the *Receita Federal*, as the developer of the initiative, would propose that colleges set up a NAF. Nowadays, due to the positive results of the existing NAFs, colleges sometimes take the initiative in contacting the *Receita Federal*.

The essence of the relationship between the *Receita Federal* and the university is moderately formal. Not all NAFs have formal written agreements: simply co-operation protocols with little juridical content. This is a very important point; a rigid instrument or overly-detailed contract would stifle colleges from creating new supporting institutions and developing innovative ideas.

The college usually organises a presentation to find motivated students. Two or three workshops then bring together students, teachers and *Receita Federal* employees. These are an opportunity for the *Receita Federal* staff to train students in key topics for their future tax studies: the use of fiscal services through the *Receita Federal*'s Internet portal, how the taxpayer databases work, regulations for small enterprises and the dynamics of the tax process in the administrative courts. Each NAF defines how it wants to assist low-income taxpayers and develops study groups based on its resources (availability of students, public, teachers, etc.). It also provides a guarantee that it will not compete with established accounting firms. A NAF may help more than 50 people every day during the busiest tax period.

Regular meetings bring the tax administration, academic community and society together. For example, students give mini-talks (approximately five minutes) to other classes in the college, acting as true "tax knowledge pollinators". They also put together their own materials (presentations, videos, etc.), one of the most important practices to emerge from the centres. Students visit tax administration offices at least once a year. They might visit public attendance units, administrative courts or units for auditing and collection, allowing them to understand and observe at first hand their routines and structure.

Impacts

- A steep and steady increase in the number of NAFs being set up: from 11 in 2011 to a total of 26 centres in 5 states today (Table 4.1). This is perhaps the most impressive result of NAFs. Most centres are in Rio Grande do Sul, where the initiative started, but many other states are coming on board. Apart from the NAF in Brasilia, which is hosted by a foreign trade faculty, all the others operate in accounting schools.
- Impressive social and media diffusion: since 2011, the various NAFs have produced 4 TV videos, more than 120 Internet releases on tax topics for the economically less-favoured, held approximately 80 talks and participated in many public fairs and open events. These numbers are likely to be conservative, since other material circulating on the Internet is not taken into account.
- Help for low-income taxpayers: the numbers of people helped by NAFs varies. One NAF in Rio Grande do Sul helped more than 50 people every day during March and April 2013, the Brazilian season for filing income tax. Other smaller centres help no more than two or three people a week.
- Growing interest and involvement: approximately 150 people (student volunteers and teachers) work in the 26 NAFs. The first regional seminar to debate the NAF initiative attracted 340 participants from various cities. While the tax administration does not control who participates in the project, it does maintain a database of collaborators for disseminating information of interest.
- Links built between the administration and citizens: the project has gained national relevance, receiving an award in the *Receita Federal*'s most prestigious contest, *Prêmio de Criatividade e Inovação* in 2011 (Bravo and Peres, 2011). This describes NAF as one of the elements in the construction of the "golden bridge" between the administration and society. The project has since become a strategic priority for the Brazilian tax administration. It is being closely observed by other countries interested in taking a similar approach to tax morality by training university students.

Lessons learnt

This project is has many positive points to be replicated, as well as challenges to overcome.

For universities, the greatest challenge is keeping up the supply of students: many work part-time in addition to their studies, therefore mechanisms are needed to keep them involved in the project. Moreover, universities have costs associated with the project: they must allocate an area for study and meetings, pay the teacher who supervises students, organise publicity and so on. Strategies to overcome such difficulties vary among institutions. A few have decided to work with first-year accounting students; this gives the students extra motivation at the beginning of their course work, while avoiding rapid attrition of graduating students.

For the tax administration, the fact that NAF centres may be supported by other tax actors, not exclusively by the *Receita Federal*, raises challenges in ensuring follow-up and the organised development of the network. Technology and knowledge management instruments are being developed to help meet this challenge. It is an exciting moment for the creation of innovative knowledge management ideas. Through NAF, trainee accountants work alongside the tax administration rather than litigating against it.

Table 4.1. **The evolution of centres for accounting and tax support in Brazil**

Number	NAF	State	Starting year
1	Anhanguera – Passo Fundo	Rio Grande do Sul	2011
2	Cesuca	Rio Grande do Sul	2011
3	FACCAT	Rio Grande do Sul	2011
4	FACOS	Rio Grande do Sul	2011
5	FEMA	Rio Grande do Sul	2011
6	IESA	Rio Grande do Sul	2011
7	IPA Metodista	Rio Grande do Sul	2011
8	Monteiro Lobato (FATO)	Rio Grande do Sul	2011
9	São Judas Tadeu	Rio Grande do Sul	2011
10	UFSM	Rio Grande do Sul	2011
11	UNIJUI	Rio Grande do Sul	2011
12	CESMAC	Alagoas	2012
13	Brasilia	Distrito Federal	2012
14	Anglicana de Erexim	Rio Grande do Sul	2012
15	Facensa	Rio Grande do Sul	2012
16	Feevale	Rio Grande do Sul	2012
17	UCS – Caxias do Sul	Rio Grande do Sul	2012
18	UCPel	Rio Grande do Sul	2012
19	UFRGS	Rio Grande do Sul	2012
20	UNISC	Rio Grande do Sul	2012
21	URI – Santiago	Rio Grande do Sul	2012
22	Coronel Fabriciano	Minas Gerais	2013
23	FADERGS	Rio Grande do Sul	2013
24	Tapejara	Rio Grande do Sul	2013
25	UCS – Nova Prata	Rio Grande do Sul	2013
26	Sorocaba	Sao Paulo	2013

Source: Secretariat of the Federal Revenue of Brazil.

Estimating the number of employees and the costs associated with the project is another challenge for the tax administration. NAF has proven to be a light project. On average, there is only one *Receita Federal* employee for every five or six centres. Their role is to help to plan events, support students with technical advice and hold courses. The interventions are well defined (meetings, talks, visits, among others) and can be divided among tax administration employees who already work at the interface with the public or in any fiscal education project. Overall, the work time spent by any tax administration unit on NAFs is minimal.

Next steps

New initiatives continue to shape the NAF idea. Recently, a few NAFs started to operate with the SAJU, helping in simple judicial cases that needed accounting or auditing reports. Other centres are experimenting with giving proactive assistance to communities in need: students set up caravans in places where there are small businesses, squatters, elderly people in need, and so on.

In sum, NAF signals an important qualitative change in the relationship between the tax administration and the accountant. The latter starts his or her career working alongside the tax administration, rather than litigating against it. This relationship derives from mutual knowledge and trust and generally strengthens the bonds between state and society.

Box 4.2. ***Receita Federal***

The *Receita Federal*'s mission is to administer tax and customs fairly and with respect for the citizen, for the benefit of the whole society. The *Receita Federal* employs 28 000 people throughout Brazil. It has a Central Unit – located in the capital, Brasilia – which comprises 5 undersecretaries and 11 direct special assistance offices. There are also decentralised units, composed of 10 regional offices, 103 judgement offices, 26 customs offices, 55 inspectorates and 362 agencies.

For more information: see the *Receita Federal* website: www.receita.fazenda.gov.br.

Source: Secretariat of the Federal Revenue of Brazil.

References

Bravo, A.M. and C.B. Peres (2011), "Construindo a ponte de ouro entre a Receita Federal do Brasil e o contribuinte: Os resultados de uma pesquisa-ação" (Constructing the golden bridge between Receita Federal and the taxpayer: The results of action research), *Administração Pública Prêmio de Criatividade e Inovação* (in Portuguese), Auditor-Fiscal da Receita Federal do Brasil José Antônio Schontag (Tax Auditor Federal Revenue and Customs Secretariat), ESAF, Brasília, available at: http://www.esaf.fazenda.gov.br/editor/resolveuid/ebbad3fdc279b57219ba00cbdba8ee60.

Receita Federal (2012), *Portaria RFB nº 896* (in Portuguese), 5 April 2012, available at: www.receita.fazenda.gov.br/Legislacao/Portarias/2012/portrfb8962012.htm.

Taxpayer Advocate Service (2013), *Low Income Taxpayer Clinics: Progress Report*, February, Department of Treasury, Washington DC, available at: www.irs.gov/pub/irs-pdf/p5066.pdf.

Chapter 5

Burundi: Reaching the informal sector

Burundi Revenue Authority

This chapter presents Burundi's taxpayer education programme. It first gives an overview of the whole programme and its objectives, followed by a focus on one specific element, the taxpayer identification number (TIN) campaign in the informal sector. It subsequently looks at the impacts and lessons learnt of the initiative, followed by an outlook on next steps.

Broadening the tax base is a high priority for Burundi. Many businesses – especially micro and small enterprises – operate in the informal sector. They are not necessarily aware of their tax obligations or the reasons for them, or the potential benefits of being integrated into the formal economy.

The Burundi Revenue Authority (OBR, *Office Burundais des Recettes*; see Box 5.3) works to address a public at times sceptical or possibly confused about why or how they should pay tax; to communicate with the business community to inform them of new ways of paying tax (and the consequences of not doing so); to remind all that corruption and tax avoidance or evasion amount to theft from the whole of society; and, along with partners in government and elsewhere, to show potential investors that a clean fiscal regime signals a government and public intent on welcoming them to Burundi.

Burundi's taxpayer education

Tax education is the task of the OBR's Taxpayer Education Section, which works hand-in-hand with the Media Section in the Communications Division. Both sections come under the umbrella of the Communication and Taxpayer Services Directorate. The Taxpayer Education Section has two staff, who deliver a range of programmes and initiatives. These are targeted at all personal income taxpayers, but especially those in a low tax bracket, the informal sector and young people (Box 5.1):

- publishing information on the OBR website
- publishing information in the local and international press
- producing many radio and television broadcasts
- organising seminars and workshops
- holding awareness-raising campaigns in shopping malls.

Box 5.1. Objectives of taxpayer education in Burundi

- Improve compliance while providing high-quality services to taxpayers.
- Explain why, and how, taxes should be paid.
- Inform the public in general, and taxpayers in particular, of innovative projects to speed up procedures for declaring and paying taxes and levies.
- Educate taxpayers on new tax legislation and other administrative measures to ensure that they understand their tax obligations.
- Raise taxpayers' awareness of the need to fight against bribery and fraud.
- Empower citizens to engage in discussions on the use of tax revenue.
- Increase the tax literacy of citizens.

Source: Burundi Revenue Authority.

Much of this work involves close partnerships with the local media; the OBR Commissioner-General meets media managers personally during quarterly "press cafés", which have become the preferred venue for meetings between the OBR and the media. Work is currently underway to set up media contracts with a range of outlets to support the OBR in its outreach activities. The choice of outlet is driven by a number of factors including audience reach, reputation and programme range.

Other partners include business organisations – notably the Federal Chamber of Commerce and Industry – and investors through TradeMark East Africa (Box 5.2). TradeMark East Africa is funded by international development agencies to enhance trade and investment in the region.

Focus on: The taxpayer identification number campaign in the informal sector

Between November 2011 and August 2012 the OBR ran an initiative to encourage informal traders to register for a taxpayer identification number (TIN), thereby bringing them into the tax net. The campaign started in shopping centres in the capital Bujumbura, and was then extended to markets and shops.

Because of the complexity of reaching this population, the taxpayer registration initiative brought together the Communication and Taxpayer Services Directorates, the Directorate for Small and Medium-Sized Taxpayers and the directorate in charge of risk management.

Burundi's public is at times sceptical and confused about why or how they should pay tax. The campaign began with general awareness-raising sessions on why taxes should be paid and to increase the tax literacy of citizens. The sessions were conducted in collaboration with local administrators and market managers, who were asked to pass on information and the announcement of an upcoming registration to respective traders. This was very important as the message was better received when conveyed by the administrative authorities than by the OBR's officials. The registration exercise was also publicly announced in press releases and on national, regional and local radio. Communication materials were developed in both French and Kirundi.

Following the general awareness-raising campaigns, a second phase was conducted in shopping malls in order to specifically raise awareness of citizens and taxpayers on the need to register as a taxpayer in order to ensure compliance with tax obligations. For this purpose, a team of 12 registration officials was recruited from students at the University of Burundi. Their job was to help traders register. Those who registered were then asked to visit the tax administration's offices in order to be issued a TIN. The OBR's officials covered shopping malls in all communes of Bujumbura quarter by quarter.

In addition to the students, the initiative involved five OBR employees. Their key role was the census of non-registered taxpayers. Total costs of the initiative are estimated at USD 30 000. Funding was obtained from TradeMark East Africa (for a support vehicle) and from the OBR.

Impacts

- An increase in taxpayer registration: while there has been no evaluation of this initiative, its success can be judged by the fact that around 7 000 new taxpayers were registered during the campaign period. They have been issued TINs. This increase in registration will boost the number of declarations for various types of tax and reduce the size of the informal sector.

- An increase in taxpayer literacy: the initiative has also helped to build taxpayers' knowledge of how to pay taxes, as well as contributing to their sense of moral obligation to pay taxes "voluntarily."
- More positive perceptions: the public appreciates that the tax administration has made a genuine effort to reach out to them. The initiative also seems to have led to a slight improvement in taxpayers' perception that they are treated fairly and transparently by the tax administration, and reassured them that other taxpayers are also paying their fair share.
- An increase in tax compliance: compliance has improved greatly over the past five years.

Lessons learnt

This initiative emphasises that involving officials who are closer to the people than the tax office – such as local authorities and traders' representatives – can be the most effective strategy for raising awareness. It is therefore very important to get the support of all stakeholders, and to involve those actors from the outset. Potential taxpayers need to be convinced of the important development role taxes play in a poor country.

For example, some local authorities and market committees were concerned that the initiative would be bad for business and needed to be persuaded in advance to facilitate OBR access. TradeMark East Africa has been an important partner in this area, helping to show local government and business representatives the important role that the tax system plays in enhancing trade and investment (Box 5.2). The OBR is taking steps to put in place a framework for collaboration with local government in order to conduct joint taxpayer awareness-raising activities throughout the country.

The biggest hurdle to overcome is convincing potential taxpayers of the important development role taxes play in a poor country. Lack of awareness of this urgent priority meant that many taxpayers failed to turn up for their appointments to fill out the TIN registration cards or simply refused to provide any information. Repeated efforts were needed to obtain their registration.

Box 5.2. Making the case for the benefits of taxes

The OBR has recently launched a new, 18-month Anti-Corruption and Communication Strategy in collaboration with TradeMark East Africa and with the support of USAID. The campaign will focus on three main areas:

1. General public education on new tax procedures as well as services available to taxpayers.
2. Disseminating anti-corruption messages and seeking support for establishing a call centre for the public to report suspected cases of corruption.
3. Disseminating information on the government's effort to improve the business regulatory environment, how tax revenues can benefit the public good and how Burundi benefits from being a member country of the East African Community (EAC).

Source: Burundi Revenue Authority.

Next steps

The next step once TINs are issued will be to explain to those newly registered how to declare and pay their taxes. The initiative will also be extended to other shopping centres in the country. Work is still in progress to reach street vendors. In 2013 with the creation of a new directorate on small and micro taxpayers, work will continue in collaboration with local authorities, paying particular attention to taxpayers located in rural areas. The OBR also plans to have a weekly presence at Bujumbura's main market and to organise a structured "round-region" tour every two months.

The initiative could be further improved with the support of the Adam Smith International consulting firm, which may provide technical assistance on educating and raising the awareness of taxpayers.

Box 5.3. Burundi Revenue Authority (OBR)

The OBR (*Office Burundais des Recettes*) is a semi-autonomous public revenue collection institution, established by law on 14 July 2009. The overall goal of establishing the OBR is to reduce poverty through better public revenue collection and an improved business environment. It also aims to be a modern tax administration contributing to the development of Burundi and its economic integration within the regional and global economy.

The OBR has 632 employees spread across 8 urban offices and 11 rural offices. Its work revolves around four strategic objectives:

1. revenue maximisation
2. enhancement of taxpayers' compliance
3. development of a competent and effective organisation
4. development of effective internal control systems and procedures.

For more information, see: www.obr.bi.

Source: Burundi Revenue Authority.

Chapter 6

Chile: An emerging online presence

Chilean Tax Service (SII)

This chapter presents Chile's taxpayer education programme. It first gives an overview of the whole programme and its objectives, followed by a focus on one specific element, the tax education online campaign. An additional section provides information on the staffing of the campaign. It subsequently looks at the impacts and lessons learnt of the initiative, followed by an outlook on next steps.

The Chilean Tax Service – *Servicio de Impuestos Internos* (SII; see Box 6.4) – sees taxpayer education as a key tool for changing Chilean perceptions of taxation, and as an investment for the long term. The Civic Tax Education Project was created in 2006 to increase awareness of the social relevance of taxes for the country. Seven years on, the programme now co-ordinates a range of taxpayer education initiatives.

Chile's taxpayer education

Operating from the department of the Deputy Directorate of Taxation (National Directorate), the Internal Tax Service Education Programme develops and co-ordinates SII taxpayer education activities. The SII's Head of Tax Education is responsible for the programme, overseeing approximately 180 tax education supervisors (Box 6.1). At the regional level, each department has managers and collaborators who also carry out regional activities.

Box 6.1. Objectives of Chile's Internal Tax Service Education Programme

- Change perceptions of taxation.
- Increase awareness of the social relevance of taxes for the country.
- Raise awareness among children as an investment for the future.

Source: Chilean Tax Service.

The focus of the programme is on providing information on tax education and teaching content, and to raise awareness among children. It achieves this through a range of initiatives:

- An educational website and web portal (featured below).
- A play, "Entering the SII Planet", which has toured various regions of the country.
- Promotional articles in specialised magazines (*Maestra Básica* and *Aula Creativa*).
- The provision of teaching material for use in the classroom.
- Television series: for example, educational episodes of the children's television programme *The Adventures of Ivo the Chinchilla*, broadcast by Chile National Television, in which Ivo and his friends develop concepts linked to citizenship and social co-existence; and the educational television series *Debut of the Gang* (2012), aimed at college students, and developed jointly with the National Customs Service (SNA) and the General Treasury of the Republic.
- School visits by public officials who explain tax to students and teachers in an informative and entertaining way.
- Extending the taxpayer education programme into secondary and higher education as part of the SII's 2011-2014 Strategic Plan.

- A taxpayer education module included in training programmes for all new SII employees and those taking on taxpayer education responsibilities, thereby assuring that taxpayer education is covered in all in-house training.

The programme has involved co-operation with key partners as a means to develop and promote a joint approach to tax education. For example, the National Television Council (CNTV) has shown its support by developing and broadcasting an audiovisual educational series.

The Ministry of Education has also reviewed primary education material and a tax education module has been included in a teachers' training course by the National Consumer Service (Sernac).

The European Union's EUROsociAL Taxation Programme has supported various initiatives, including exchanges among Latin American countries to learn from regional experience in implementing tax education initiatives (see Chapters 8 and 9 for examples).

Focus on: Tax education online

This educational initiative, launched by the taxpayer education programme in 2006, consists of two educational web portals: SIIEduca and Planeta SII. Both are freely accessible and together represent two of the main instruments of the taxpayer education programme.

The first website, SIIEduca, is aimed at teachers, parents and tutors as well as the general public. It provides information on taxpayer education and offers content suggestions for teachers and tutors (Box 6.2). The second website, Planeta SII, is directed at primary schoolchildren (6-13 years old) and their teachers (Box 6.3). It presents its teaching material in an entertaining manner, whilst reinforcing civic responsibility and values. Students are taught, for instance, about the importance of solidarity, teamwork and complying with local government. This, along with issues relevant to taxation, provides students with content relevant to their everyday lives which teachers may use to reinforce their syllabus with cross-cutting tax content.

Box 6.2. SIIEduca: A resource for teachers

- A web portal specifically devoted to teachers.
- All teachers have access to relevant material and good educational practice relating to tax matters.
- Information on subjects (classes) is included for each year of primary education (Years 1 to 8), with class schedules for the first cycle of primary education and suggested syllabi for the second cycle.
- Material is provided for college students; particularly technical and professional college education, and includes modules on tax education, small business management and commercial and tax regulations. Particular attention is paid to entrepreneurship.
- Children's content is reinforced through games available at Planeta SII.
- The use of the Internet is encouraged by bringing new technologies into the classroom.

- Links are included to social networks, news and videos.

For more information, see: www.siieduca.cl.

Source: Chilean Tax Service.

The Planeta SII site effectively combines education and entertainment in an attractive way for children through a large range of games and videos; entertaining classes; and fun and friendly characters, such as Maite, Gaspar and Ivo. It also makes use of popular Hip-Hop music, is visually engaging and has an instantly appealing homepage set out with easy to understand, clear language. On the children's website, the tax message is secondary to entertainment value.

Box 6.3. **Planeta SII: Tax fun for children**

- A website specifically aimed at children (6-13 years old). It contains entertaining content to help children learn through play (games, videos, songs and a mascot, Ivo the Chinchilla).
- Works with cross-cutting themes of value-based and civic education, where the tax content – tax type, rates, etc. – is integrated but secondary to the entertainment value.
- Divided into two stages, with varying levels of difficulty for different age groups.
- Games are in line with the teaching schedules provided by SIIEduca.
- Encourages respect for the environment as Ivo the Chinchilla represents an endangered species. This cross-cutting theme is ultimately directed at the protection of national heritage and public assets.

For more information, see: www.planetasii.cl.

Source: Chilean Tax Service.

Both websites have been developed further over time. In 2012, they were redesigned to improve usability and to allow for their integration into social networking. In 2013, material for college students was added, thereby reaching a previously untargeted demographic group.

External companies have collaborated in creating the sites, including design specialists and experts in drafting educational material. These services were procured through external tender proceedings which specified the need for education, design and communications professionals. The Ministry of Education sponsored the review and distribution of primary education material.

During the development stage, an alliance was established with Educarchile to index the website contents of the programme. Educarchile is a privately sponsored, independent and pluralist web portal that acts as a public service, with collaboration from the public and private sectors. Educarchile does work for all members of the national education community: schools, teachers, students and principals; Chilean families and parent and tutor institutions; municipal and private sponsors; educational research and specialists; as well as university faculties of education and cultural organisations.

Staffing the taxpayer education campaign

Many of the 180 tax education supervisors provide valuable ideas and suggestions for the websites. They are supported by an internal designer, two computer technicians, an administrative assistant and a site manager. Their roles are described in Table 6.1.

There are five external employees in total including a teacher, an educational psychologist, a methodological counsellor, a web designer and a computer programmer.

Regional managers and supervisors are given training before visiting schools and delivering presentations to publicise the sites and available material.

Table 6.1. **Staff roles in tax education in Chile**

Tax education supervisors	Talks and regional visits to publicise the websites and their material
Head of Tax Education Programme	Co-ordination of various activities, drafting proposals, tender proceedings, planning, etc.
Public officials in the programme area	Collaboration at meetings, drawing up of proposals, review of material, product testing
Internal design support	Graphics and design for the programme
Computer support	Technical support and product development; installation of trial servers and providing Internet access
Administrative assistance	Drawing up of tender bases and awarding proposals
Site manager	Senior maintenance manager relating to tenders, opinions and questions, and social networks
External staff, tendered companies	Drawing up of material and proposals subject to technical, design and syllabus requirements

Source: Chilean Tax Service.

Table 6.2. **Approximate costs of the tax education initiative in Chile**

	Chilean peso	USD	Exchange Rate
2006 (Stage 1)	17 million	32 056	530.33 CLP/USD
2008 (Stage 2)	33 million	63 222	521.97 CLP/USD
2009 (Maintenance)	2 million	3 574	559.67 CLP/USD
2011 (Redesign)	4 million	8 267	483.84 CLP/USD
2012 (Stage 3)	2 million	4 109	486.89 CLP/USD
Total	58 million	111 228	

Source: Chilean Tax Service.

Impacts

The SII views tax education as a long-term investment, expecting results to be seen in future generations. However, with the planned inclusion of tax education in secondary and higher levels of education, the period for results should be shorter, as the students will soon graduate, obliging them to make decisions about their civic duties and tax.

An assessment conducted by an independent company – Adimark – of the perceptions of primary education children found that:

- Children and teachers appreciate the Planeta SII site: children between six and nine years of age were positive about the educational and entertainment value of the site. Teachers also found the site both entertaining and educational and generally gave positive feedback, valuing the importance that SII placed on civic education.

- The sites are useful teaching resources: teachers noted that the sites conform well to their work methodologies in the teaching environment and provide them with information about taxes that they had not known before.
- Tax officials find the sites useful: it adds a new dimension to their work, whilst also instilling a strong feeling of social commitment to the work they do for their country.
- The sites help change perceptions: the sites helped teachers view and interpret taxation from a different perspective and they were able to work this into their daily role as educators. These ideas were easily incorporated into the syllabus, rather than being "an additional burden".
- The sites prompt more positive views of the SII's educational work and of its concern for citizen issues.

Please note that the study was conducted during the trial phase of the website in the first half of 2006. These results were used to make modifications to the site including adjustments in content and navigation that enabled the SII to proceed to the official nationwide launch, which occurred in November 2006.

In August 2012, Chile's Queveo Foundation granted the 2012 Queveo Prize to www.planetasii.cl in the Children's Internet category for its contribution to civic education. This annual award recognises television programmes, websites, advertisements and educational digital initiatives that promote social values such as respect, tolerance, responsibility, perseverance and discernment, amongst others.

Lessons learnt

The Tax Education Programme's educational websites have become fundamental tools for strengthening the tax content in various areas. This is particularly so in schools, where taxpayer education is viewed as essential.

The main challenge for this initiative is keeping the online content and navigation platform up to date and relevant. Because the programme encourages follow-up work and new challenges, there is a need for regular new material. Added to this is the ever-changing face of technology. All of this means that strategic and periodic reviews are essential in order for this project to remain dynamic, attractive and relevant to its target demographic (through the use of mobile video sections, news, tenders and so forth).

Next steps

In addition to the continuous updating and monitoring of social networks mentioned above, during 2013 the programme was to gradually add material for college students, giving priority to professional and technical education. The challenge was to generate enough material by 2014 to cover all tertiary levels, with topics including entrepreneurship, innovation and the importance of not operating in the informal economy.

Box 6.4. The Chilean Tax Service

The Chilean Tax Service (SII) is one of the state's taxation institutions under the National Directorate of Taxation. The SII's aim is to maximise and facilitate compliance with voluntary tax payments. This is achieved by providing services in an efficient, equitable and transparent manner, making accessible to the population the means by which to achieve this. The work is executed by competent and committed public officials. It has a total of 4 184 staff, distributed across the National Directorate, 18 regional departments, 50 units (in regional departments) and a Large Taxpayers' Division.

For more information:

Website: www.sii.cl

E-mail address of the tax education programme: portaleducativo@sii.cl

Source: Chilean Tax Service.

Chapter 7

Colombia: Digital signature and online declarations

National Directorate of Taxes and Customs

This chapter presents Colombia's taxpayer education programme. It first gives an overview of the whole programme and its objectives, followed by a focus on one specific element, the digital signature and online filing campaign. It finally looks at the impacts and lessons learnt of the initiative.

Colombia's Ministry of Public Finance and the National Directorate of Taxes and Customs (DIAN; Box 7.2) recognise the systemic challenges facing the country and the role of the tax system in addressing some of them. In 2012, Colombia began a comprehensive tax reform. Its main objectives are to: encourage formalisation of employment through reduced labour costs; reduce inequality through progressive income taxation; simplify value-added tax (VAT) tariffs; increase tax revenues in the medium term through pro-growth and pro-formalisation measures; and reduce tax evasion by providing new anti-avoidance measures.

The DIAN helps to ensure Colombia's fiscal security and protect national economic public order by administering and enforcing tax, customs and exchange regulations. It shares joint responsibility for tax reform and tax policy with the Ministry of Public Finance. It also works with the Ministry of Commerce to lobby for tax compliance by private sector organisations. Key communication roles include interpreting tax legislation and communicating with taxpayers (Box 7.1).

Colombia's taxpayer education

Responsibility for taxpayer education is integrated within several of the DIAN's departments and agencies. However, a key player is the Communications Office, which is responsible for developing strategies and campaigns. It ensures user-friendly language in all publications and provides information on taxpayer obligations, legal sanctions, negative effects on society of tax avoidance and the benefits of tax compliance.

Box 7.1. Objectives of taxpayer education in Colombia

- Promote social acceptance of taxes.
- Foster a tax-paying culture.
- Provide citizens with guidance and up-to-date information about rules, procedures and the tools at their disposal to help them meet their tax, customs and currency exchange obligations.
- Show citizens how to pay taxes.
- Explain why taxes should be paid.
- Increase the number of citizens who pay taxes.
- Empower citizens to engage in discussions on the use of tax revenue.
- Increase the tax literacy of citizens.

Source: National Directorate of Taxes and Customs.

Specific activities include:

- developing dedicated websites for each type of tax or levy, to provide taxpayers with all the information they need to meet their tax obligations
- press and social media campaigns to promote social acceptance of taxation and inform taxpayers and customs users on how to easily meet their tax obligations
- seminars and workshops

- production of teaching booklets on taxes for secondary and elementary schools
- contests and awards
- video conferences
- preparation of digital guides, booklets, services and other information.

The DIAN's taxpayer education activities are targeted at:

- all personal income taxpayers
- all corporate income taxpayers
- the informal sector
- people displaced as a result of violence
- young people, especially young entrepreneurs
- community action groups participating in social service fairs and other forms of association.

The DIAN has two employees fully dedicated to research on taxpayer education. Their work includes targeting strategies for the various groups around the country and timing campaigns throughout the tax year. They also assess the impact of taxpayer education activities and changes in taxpayer perceptions.

The DIAN has also worked closely with the Ministry of Education on taxpayer education in schools. Currently the DIAN partners with schools in the capital of Bogotá directly. Partnerships with the media are managed by the Media Centrum, which manages contracts centrally. The DIAN also works with business organisations and civil society organisations. Partnerships with trade associations are established mainly on request by the business organisations for workshops and training. Another important partner is the EUROsociAL project, which supports various taxpayer education activities.

Focus on: Digital signature and online filing campaign

Digital signatures make tax filing easy and secure. The digital signature is a mechanism created by the DIAN to allow taxpayers to sign their online tax declaration and file their information safely. It is now obligatory for all large firms. This tool increases taxpayer compliance by making the tax filing process as easy as possible: there is no need to print forms for signing or to go to the bank.

The DIAN launched an information campaign to show business taxpayers the benefits of using a digital signature and how to go about it. This included making all new clients aware that they can file declarations online using the digital signature, and explaining that they must first register for a taxpayer identification number before applying for a digital signature.

The campaign's specific objectives were to:

- increase compliance by building confidence in the security of online instruments
- teach people how to pay taxes

- raise citizens' "tax literacy".

The Digital Signature Mechanism seeks to target as many taxpayers as possible:

- those classified by the DIAN as high tax bracket taxpayers
- public notaries
- consortiums and joint ventures
- foreign exchange market intermediaries
- postal services concessionaires that provide postal financial services
- holders of settlement current accounts that are required to file foreign exchange and foreign indebtedness information with the DIAN
- taxpayers who opt to issue electronic invoices
- DIAN officials who are required to file declarations
- taxpayers authorised and awarded concessions to operate games of chance and gambling offered by government-owned entities nationwide
- taxpayers required to file individual and consolidated transfer price declarations
- representatives, tax auditors and accountants of taxpayers required to file the electronic declarations as indicated above.

The campaign involved mass communication using high-impact media such as national, regional and local radio and newspapers, and social media such as Facebook and Twitter. It also used text messages, phone calls, letters and emails to directly contact registered taxpayers who are required to use the digital signature.

A questionnaire in newspapers and on the DIAN's web page allowed clients to determine whether or not they are required to file declarations online. Technical guides were also developed for users on how to file declarations, send information electronically and use the digital signature.

The DIAN had four employees involved at the national level to co-ordinate the campaign itself. However, the implementation of the digital signature mechanism, technology development and customer support involved a total of 550 employees (500 in the Customer Service Department nationwide, including 150 employees at the central level and 150 in the call centre). Staff needed to be trained in the new tax procedures. This training was not specific to tax officials and was conducted jointly with customer education. The total costs of the campaign were approximately COP 100 million (USD 530 000).

Several other partners were involved in the campaign: government departments and agencies, various media, business organisations, chambers of commerce and civil society members.

Impacts

- An increase in online declarations: while there has been no independent evaluation of the initiative, the number of taxpayers filing their declarations online reached 360 000; exceeding the DIAN's goal of 250 000 by 110 000 taxpayers. However, as taxpayers are obliged to file online, this achievement cannot solely be attributed to the taxpayer education campaign. To date, the initiative has reached approximately 620 000 taxpayers.

- An increase in voluntary compliance: the digital signature initiative is also considered to be a success as it has not only helped increase the tax base, but also the level of voluntary compliance. It demonstrates that citizens' social acceptance of taxes plays an essential role in controlling tax evasion, including increasing the number of people reporting tax evaders to the DIAN.
- An increase in taxpayer literacy: there has been a marked improvement in the skills required to pay taxes, and especially in the use of the electronic information system. For example, in 2012, eight times more digital signatures were activated than in 2011, most of them online. However, the increase in people's sense of moral obligation to pay taxes "voluntarily" is not as great as desired.

The campaign and the high number of online activations of digital signatures showed taxpayers that the tax administration is trying to simplify procedures for them and avoid unnecessary personal visits to the tax office.

Lessons learnt

A key challenge has been the lack of a "computer culture" among citizens. This problem was resolved by providing customer support with the help of the Ministry of Information and Communications Technologies. For example, kiosks were established for personalised self-service.

A second problem was that the DIAN's technology is outdated and often not compatible with the software used by companies. This causes huge problems for customers, who have to keep an outdated computer to be able to comply with the law. The DIAN is currently updating all web profiles and setting up a lighter IT validating system, making use of new technologies. This process, however, will only be finalised in 2018. New options for registration and authentication of signatures are being developed, including a simplified regime for taxpayers. Furthermore, the digital signature mechanism has been extended to new groups of taxpayers.

Box 7.2. Colombia's National Directorate of Taxes and Customs (DIAN)

The DIAN (*Dirección De Impuestos Y Aduanas Nacionales*) was set up in 1993 as a special administrative unit and is legally independent, has administrative and budgetary autonomy, and its own assets. It is accountable to the Ministry of Public Finance. The DIAN consists of a Head Office, Tax Division, Customs Division, secretariats, Advisory and Co-ordination Offices and agencies, all accountable to the Office of the Director General. It has 1 000 employees in its central office in the capital Bogota, and there are also 6 regional administration offices each with their own delegate and local administrative offices, sometimes dealing with both tax and customs. For more information:

- Website: www.dian.gov.co
- Facebook: www.facebook.com/pages/DIAN-Direcci%C3%B3n-de-Impuestos-y-Aduanas-Nacionales/152427691450232?v=wall
- Twitter: https://twitter.com/#!/DIANColombia

Source: National Directorate of Taxes and Customs.

Chapter 8

Costa Rica: The "Tribute to My Country" games room

General Directorate of Taxation (DGT)

This chapter presents Costa Rica's taxpayer education programme. It first gives an overview of the whole programme and its objectives, followed by a focus on one specific element, the "Tribute to My Country" games room. It finally looks at the impacts of the initiative and gives an outlook on next steps.

Tax education in Costa Rica is regarded as a matter of public interest, reflecting a national commitment to creating a positive tax culture in the country (Box 8.1). The General Directorate of Taxation (*Dirección General de Tributación* or DGT; Box 8.3) focuses on encouraging voluntary compliance and striking a balance between public obligation, rights and taxpayer guarantees.

Over the last ten years, the DGT has developed an innovative approach to tax education, with an emphasis on informing citizens of the social role of taxation: a citizen who is convinced is also committed to paying his/her taxes and cares for public assets.

Exchanges with Argentina and El Salvador helped Costa Rica set up its Tax Education and Culture Programme. Costa Rica began developing its tax education strategy by putting together a group of public officials to work on tax education and culture. Technical and financial assistance was requested from the European Union and Latin America Co-operation Programme EUROsociAL Taxation (between 2005 and 2010). The members of the Tax Education and Culture group were trained by Argentina's Federal Administration for Public Revenue (AFIP). The group visited the AFIP as well as El Salvador's Tax Education Unit in the Ministry of Finance. This culminated in Costa Rica setting up its own Taxpayer Education Unit in 2010. The responsibility for taxpayer education activities falls under the Sub-Directorate for Tax Education and Culture, which was created in 2010 within the DGT's Directorate of Taxpayer Services.

Costa Rica's taxpayer education

Key activities include:

- Tax Education Week, which is a regular fixture on the school calendar, organised with the Ministry of Public Education
- training primary and secondary school teachers, including through the National University, to apply tax education across the educational syllabus
- running tax culture courses for all tax offices
- running basic taxation courses for accounting students at technical schools to encourage awareness of their future responsibilities.

Box 8.1. Objectives of Costa Rica's taxpayer education

- Encourage citizen awareness of the importance of taxes for the country.
- Inform citizens of the social role of taxation.
- Establish a close relationship with citizens.
- Teach children the importance of paying taxes in relation to fundamental concepts and values such as solidarity, co-operation and citizen responsibility.
- Inform the student population of tax matters.

Source: General Directorate of Taxation.

Focus on: "Tribute to My Country" games room

The "Tribute to My Country" games room is an attractive and entertaining space for teaching young children the importance of taxation. Inaugurated in 2010, it is located in one of the country's main attractions for children: the *Museo de los Niños* in the capital city, San José. This large room (120 m^2) includes 18 interactive devices which teach tax-related subjects through games. There are three different themes:

1. an introduction to taxation: history and origin and the most relevant taxes
2. the Legislative Assembly (one of the three powers of the republic): where and how the national budget is approved and distributed
3. tax investment and the function of customs authorities.

Some of the exhibits in the games room are described in Box 8.2.

Box 8.2. Examples of games and exhibits

"The Ministry of Finance" includes a video game entitled "Tax Statements" which involves completing a tax income statement in a user-friendly format, entering basic details. The aim is for children to become familiar with tax payments and the taxation cycle. This space represents the electronic service points located at tax administrations.

"*La Facturita*" (The Little Invoice Shop) teaches about the general tax levied on sales. By pretending to buy and sell, children learn how this tax works: how to distinguish which payment receipts are valid and which are not. They are also encouraged to get used to requesting an invoice.

In the "Public Money Path and the Legislative Assembly" space, children learn about the budget and how it is distributed, as well as how tax money is allocated to meet the country's various needs. Children pretend to be legislators and distribute taxation money amongst various items such as education, health and infrastructure.

The "Airport and Port Customs" game includes an airport scanner, which checks luggage to verify whether or not its content is legal; and a container ship. Visitors must find forbidden products, both for import and export.

Source: General Directorate of Taxation.

The space and teaching content were jointly conceived by taxpayer education specialists from the AFIP (Argentina), the curators of the *Museo de los Niños* and the national tax education team.

The main objective of this room is to build a positive tax culture amongst the children of Costa Rica through entertaining devices to teach:

- the value of taxes for the common good of the country
- what taxes are and what they mean for progress
- the tax cycle
- the basic concepts of allocating state resources through the national budget
- the social investment made by the state to benefit Costa Rican society.

The games room offers free or guided visits by museum guides who take visitors through the activities and answer any questions. These guides are trained by staff from the Sub-Directorate for Tax Education and Culture, who passed on knowledge and information learned from their exchange trips to Argentina and El Salvador. By June 2013, 21 training sessions had been held and 223 guides were qualified. In 2012, to mark the 95th anniversary of the General Directorate of Taxation, a series of guided visits were offered to children and relatives of directorate employees, with the employees sharing their experience in an entertaining manner while teaching the relevance of taxation.

The museum advertises itself throughout the year, encouraging Costa Ricans to visit the games room with particular emphasis on Children's Day, holidays and its anniversary. In addition, whenever the *Museo de los Niños* arranges special events, the Sub-Directorate for Tax Education and Culture launches promotions in order to attract visitors. The Tax Administration helps, sending internal communications to its employees, advertising the games room on its website and social media, and whenever Tax Education and Culture staff visit schools or conduct teacher training they issue invitations to the games room.

The design, construction, assembly and initial maintenance of the room required a co-operation agreement between the Ministry of Finance, CEDDET-EUROsociAL Taxation and the *Ayúdenos para Ayudar* Foundation (*Museo de los Niños*), regulating the function and responsibility of the parties involved.

In total, the initiative has required 24 employees (from the Ministry of Finance, the AFIP [Argentina], the *Museo de los Niños* and EUROsociAL Taxation). The DGT staff managed and co-ordinated the project, while the AFIP staff, the museum's curators and Tax Education and Culture staff were in charge of defining the exhibits, components and thematic contents of the play area. They also helped with the educational and thematic content of all the games. A Costa Rican architect constructed the room and its devices, while another national company took on the graphic design of both the façade and all components and museographic modules included in each section of the "Tribute to My Country" games room.

The construction costs came to approximately CRC 32 million (around USD 65 000) and, on average, CRC 5.5 million (approximately USD 11 100) are spent each year on maintenance.

Impacts

The games room has not been evaluated independently but the exhibition is still being visited and enjoyed by thousands of children (Table 8.1).

Table 8.1. **Number and type of visitors to the *Museo de los Niños*, Costa Rica, 2010-13**

Year	Age group: under 3	Age group: ages 3-15	Age group: adults	Age group: elderly	Guests	Others	Total
2010	3 985	79 399	96 947	1 721	2 920	5 927	190 899
2011	8 745	87 560	118 195	1 906	8 198	7 414	232 018
2012	8 708	85 478	109 726	1 665	2 623	8 502	216 702
2013*	2 962	24 242	34 294	675	1 087	1 171	64 431
Total	24 400	276 679	359 162	5 967	14 828	23 014	704 050

Note: * For this period, the cut-off line was May 2013.

Source: Summary data taken from statistics issued by the Department of Operations, Reservations Office, Museo de los Niños, May 2013.

- Raised awareness: children learn through play and in an experimental and practical setting. Apart from learning about taxation and its role in society, the games room allows children to develop skills ranging from communication and collaboration to creativity and teamwork. While playing, children gradually become familiar with the concepts surrounding the need to pay tax. In addition to reaching the younger population through this space, their accompanying adults also become familiar with the room's subject matter.
- Perception changes: the initiative is an effective way of allowing educators, children and young citizens to understand the importance of paying taxes. A positive change has been observed among educators in how they perceive citizen responsibility and the relevance of taxation for the development of society.

Next steps

Recently, the Ministry of Public Education (MEP) has begun to show interest in tax education. It is expanding the games room idea into schools by providing more and more spaces for tax education in primary and secondary study programmes.

As of 2013, any teachers trained under the education initiative "200 Plan," which includes this project, will also act as promoters. This will multiply the dissemination effect, allowing tax education to reach even more educators. Furthermore, there is a proposal as part of the reform of the Social and Civic Studies Programme to include tax education as a subject in year six (primary school).

Box 8.3. General Directorate of Taxation (DGT)

The DGT (*Dirección General de Tributación*) comes under the Ministry of Finance. Its mission is: "To provide an internal tax collection service required by the state, through effective management that controls and enables compliance with tax obligations held by taxpayers and the general population, further to the application of established laws and regulations, thereby encouraging the country's economic development".

Its responsibilities are to collect and levy all internal taxes. It employs 992 public officials (34% of all staff employed by the Ministry of Finance). In addition to a head office, it has ten tax offices across the country.

For more information, see: Education and Tax Culture website: http://educa.hacienda.go.cr:8080/costarica_prod.

Source: General Directorate of Taxation.

Chapter 9

El Salvador: The Tax Education Diploma – Teaching teachers to teach tax

General Directorate of Internal Taxation

This chapter presents El Salvador's taxpayer education programme. It first gives an overview of the whole programme and its objectives, followed by a focus on one specific element, the Tax Education Diploma. It subsequently looks at the impacts and lessons learnt of the initiative, followed by an outlook on next steps.

El Salvador collects one of the lowest levels of tax revenue in Latin America (14.3% in 2009), well below the regional average (ECLAC, 2012). The Ministry of Finance, through the General Directorate of Internal Taxation (DGII; Box 9.1), has launched various activities to increase tax revenues. One of its most effective initiatives was to approve the Taxation Code in 2001, which significantly increased revenues from internal taxation. Subsequent tax reforms strengthened the tax code, while supervision and sanctioning procedures were also increased and strengthened.

It was not until 2008 that the Ministry of Finance complemented these enforcement approaches with a strategy to achieve a cultural shift in how taxes are viewed in El Salvador.

This was the goal of the European Union's EUROsociAL Taxation Programme, which supported a tax education programme in El Salvador through a pilot project in 2008-09. This provided the technical and financial support to build the foundations of the current programme. As part of this pilot project, Argentina's Department of Tax Education at the Federal Administration of Public Revenues (AFIP), which already had ten-years' experience in tax education, became a reference around which to shape an action plan for El Salvador's tax education programme.

A Tax Education Programme Unit was set up within DGII in 2009. This unit also acts as an inter-institutional link between the Ministry of Finance and the Ministry of Education. Since then, tax education has become a fundamental pillar of the Ministry of Finance and is now one of its public policies for achieving its 2009-2014 Five-Year Plan.

Box 9.1. **General Directorate of Internal Taxation (DGII)**

The DGII's main tasks are to apply and enforce all those laws on taxation, including tax rates and tax contributions, assigned to the General Directorate by law. Its main activities include:

- taxpayer assistance, receipt and processing of any tax statements
- taxpayer registration and control
- the issue of resolutions to varying degrees.

The DGII has 1 100 employees spread around 80 urban/rural offices of the Ministry of Finance. There is one General Director, a General Sub Director, an Administrative Manager and 26 staff or advisory units, including the Tax Education Unit.

For more information:

Website: www.mh.gob.sv and www.edufis.mh.gob.sv

E-mail address of the tax education programme: edufis@mh.gob.sv

Source: General Directorate of Internal Taxation.

El Salvador's taxpayer education

El Salvador has a huge range of taxpayer education activities. Many involve formal teaching approaches, while others are less formal.

- Since 2009, tax education subjects have been included in Ministry of Education's study programmes.

- A Tax Education Diploma for teachers and students of mid-level technical education (junior college).
- Tax education workshops for pre-school, basic and general mid-level educators. These generate teachers' awareness of the social relevance of taxation and provide teaching guides and materials for teaching tax education study programmes.
- Courses and university forums for general mid-level, technical mid-level and university students on the social relevance of taxation.
- In-house training for Ministry of Finance employees on the social significance of taxation and the various tax education activities available.
- Training for employees in other public and private institutions to encourage awareness amongst public officials or taxpayers in the private sector of the social relevance of taxation.
- Professional training on the social relevance of taxation for students (future public officials) in the Ministry of Finance's Human Talent Programme.

Box 9.2. **Objectives of taxpayer education in El Salvador**

- Complement enforcement with awareness.
- Bring about a cultural shift in how taxes are viewed.
- Cultivate social values, citizenship and tax culture.

Source: General Directorate of Internal Taxation.

The Tax Education Programme Unit has created the *RecreHacienda*! and *Exprésate* activity centres as fun spaces where children and teenagers can learn the social relevance of taxation through games and recreational activities. A programme called *RecreHacienda*! Under the Sun brings Tax Education Unit staff to educational centres where they arrange open-air group events on tax culture. Ministry of Finance staff also visit schools to carry out entertaining and educational activities.

Plays are put on in the theatre to change perceptions and improve tax culture. Information stands, tax education bulletins and informative cards are other techniques used.

Focus on: The Tax Education Diploma

The Tax Education Diploma, launched in 2009, trains accounting and business teachers and students in mid-level technical education (junior college), both on-site and online. This joint strategy of the Ministries of Education and Finance aims to improve the tax literacy of technical mid-level college teachers, who then share their knowledge with their students, parents, principals, relatives and teaching colleagues. The Tax Education Diploma involves a technical component, enabling teachers to integrate tax issues into all subjects they teach. It applies the three foundations, or pillars, on which tax education is based: values, citizenship and tax culture.

Technical subjects – such as updates to the tax code, personal income tax and value-added tax (VAT) – are taught to teachers during eight online courses through the Moodle distance learning platform, www.edufis.mh.gob.sv. Each week the online work sets different reading material and each participant is required to answer a questionnaire, to participate in various forums and to complete tasks required by the online tutor. At the end of each week the participant's work is graded.

In 2012, the online Tax Diploma module was implemented for students in other educational centres. Accounting and business teachers participating in the diploma programme who had obtained outstanding grades became online tutors for new participants.

The diploma operates through a partnership between the Ministry of Education and the educational centres. The Ministry of Education draws up an annual operating plan for the diploma. It reviews the material to be published in each diploma programme, designs appraisals for each course, supervises participants and accompanies Ministry of Finance staff to any on-site course. It is the role of the educational centres to encourage teachers or students to participate in the diploma programme, to help arrange and run Tax Culture Week (Box 9.3) and to help teachers or students use computers during the online course.

Several technicians provide permanent support to graduate students (one from the Ministry of Education, two from the Ministry of Finance and four part-time trainers). Overall, three departments in the Ministry of Education and five in the Ministry of Finance are involved. Staff participating in the initiative are trained both in on-site and online education.

Staff costs are USD 10 000 for every graduate trained through the eight courses (estimated average value based on the technical staff time spent assisting diploma students, operators and administrative staff).

Box 9.3. Tax Culture Week

This activity was initially created to ensure that teachers shared with their students all their updated tax knowledge. With the involvement of the educational community, including parents, Tax Culture Week uses the three pillars of tax education (training in values, construction of citizenship and tax culture) to teach taxpayers about the importance of demanding purchase receipts, caring for public spaces, citizen participation, official reports to control tax evasion, the rendering of accounts, etc. This activity also involves the implementation of educational actions launched by students through social networks (such as Facebook and Twitter).

Some educational centres arrange parades along the local streets, raffles involving the verification of formal requirements imposed on receipts and invoices, fashion shows with clothing made of VAT documents (invoices and receipts), discussions on the rendering of accounts with municipal mayors, etc. These actions require a high level of logistics and involvement on the part of the educational community.

One task assigned to participants – checking purchase documents (invoices and receipts) to discourage informal economic activity – generates an average of 1 000 reports of non-compliance during the first two days of Tax Culture Week activities.

Source: General Directorate of Internal Taxation.

Impacts

Each Tax Education Diploma graduate is assessed, allowing the Tax Education Diploma Programme to improve each year. Various quantitative evaluations are also conducted of each course to assess learning and the participants' commitment to tax culture. These evaluations are carried out by the Tax Education Unit and supervised by Ministry of Education representatives, who subsequently evaluate the academic competences involved in the Mid-Level Technical Education Programme (Business or Accounting Assistance option). In turn, the Ministry of Education receives the input of teachers and students participating in the diploma programme.

To date, the main results of the Tax Education Diploma programme include the following:

- A large number of teachers trained in tax education: 629 teachers of technical accounting college subjects are now Tax Education Diploma graduates, representing 70% of the teaching sector in this specialty.
- A large number of students learning about tax: 150 960 business students have been taught tax education by their teachers. These students may now offer better services when joining the job market due to their up-to-date tax knowledge and enhanced entrepreneurial skills. Should they decide to set up their own business, they possess basic knowledge of the relevance of voluntary tax compliance for the country's progress.
- Strengthened inter-institutional ties: the exchange of technical resources between the Ministries of Education and Finance in planning and implementing the diploma has enabled tax education to be included in fourth-, fifth- and sixth-grade study programmes and, since 2012, in the study programmes at mid-level technical colleges.
- Perception changes: El Salvador's Tax Education Programme has had an important impact on citizens, promoting behavioural change through entertaining and educational strategies directed at children, adolescents, university students, teachers, public officials and professionals, amongst others. One sign of changing perceptions is that programme participants are now organising their own tax education events, thereby enhancing the wider impact on national communities. A good example is Tax Culture Week (Box 9.3).
- Uptake of the approach by other disciplines: in another indication of a change in perceptions, many teachers in other disciplines are showing an interest in participating in the Tax Education Diploma Programme. This has encouraged the Ministries of Tax and Education to consider a pilot project for Tax Education Diploma graduates aimed at teachers and students in other disciplines, which was to commence in July 2013.

The Ministry of Finance's efforts were acknowledged in 2011 by the Secretariat for Strategic Affairs (Presidency of the Republic of El Salvador), when it was awarded first prize for its Tax Education Programme. It was also recognised for best practice in ES-CALIDAD, a national quality award that celebrates excellence achieved in the management of public and private organisations.

Lessons learnt

The main challenges encountered included:

- Scarce inter-institutional human resources to assist Tax Education Diploma graduates on-site and online.
- Internet access difficulties by teachers and participating students: despite this the drop-out rate in the diploma programme during the online stage was less than 10%.
- An initial fear of using technological tools for training: this initial fear was overcome once they had had their first online lesson.
- The Tax Education Diploma demands additional effort by both teachers and students; initially it was viewed as a very demanding responsibility. However, the wish to learn and the methodologies and duration of the programme have ensured satisfactory completion.

Next steps

Improvements planned for the future include the following:

- to extend the coverage of educational institutions, teachers and students, in various specialities and educational levels
- to further strengthen inter-ministerial communication processes
- to measure the impact of the programme and of the Tax Education Diploma
- to continue to improve the Tax Education Diploma as needs and demands gradually arise
- to strengthen study plans and programmes, such as introducing tax education just after pre-school.

Reference

ECLAC (UN Economic Commission for Latin America and the Caribbean) (2012), *Tax Structure and Tax Evasion in Latin America*, ECLAC, Santiago.

Chapter 10

Estonia: The e-Tax/e-Customs Initiative

Estonian Tax and Customs Board (ETCB)

This chapter presents Estonia's taxpayer education programme. It first gives an overview of the whole programme and its objectives, followed by a focus on one specific element, the e-Tax/e-Customs Initiative. It finally looks at the impacts and lessons learnt of the initiative.

Marketing and promoting the activities of the Estonian Tax and Customs Board (ETCB; Box 10.3) are essential to keep taxpayers aware of tax collection generally, of how taxes are used to provide public services and of what taxpayers get from paying taxes. As tax collecting and paying taxes have always been unpopular activities, the challenge for the tax authority is to change attitudes by providing top quality services and fair, straightforward communication (Box 10.1).

Estonia is one of the most "networked" countries in the world in terms of Internet use and access. The ETCB reflects and responds to this in its outreach to taxpayers.

Estonia's taxpayer education

While the ETCB does not have a separate unit for dealing with taxpayer education, different departments educate taxpayers within their specific areas.

Box 10.1. Objectives of Estonia's taxpayer education

- Make taxpayers aware of tax collection, of how taxes are essential for providing public services and of what taxpayers get from paying taxes.
- Change attitudes by providing top quality services and fair, straightforward communication.

Source: Estonian Tax and Customs Board.

The ETCB has a range of activities, systems and processes to help taxpayers understand and fulfil their tax obligations, and make interaction with the ETCB easy, fast and streamlined. It also provides high-quality tax-related information and training. This is facilitated through innovative means of communication, the development of e-services and new training options. Some examples include:

- Workshops, seminars and presentations. The ETCB offers free training workshops and seminars to taxpayers on specific tax topics. Face-to-face workshops are provided for longer and more complex tax subjects whilst web-based presentations using YouTube give brief overviews of specific topics. For example, between January and May 2013 56 workshops and seminars were held and 7 web-based presentations were posted on the ETCB website.
- Discussion forum. There is a page available on the ETCB Internet site for forum discussions. The public can post questions about tax issues and the ETCB provides answers and comments.
- Campaigns. Posters and brochures are distributed widely in the community to educate taxpayers about specific tax issues. Radio and television advertising is also used when appropriate. Usually posters and brochures are in Estonian and Russian so that information can reach most of the population.
- Social media. The ETCB has a Facebook page and a Twitter account to stream information to taxpayers quickly.
- One-to-one education at service bureaus. Estonia has 16 service bureaus (tax offices) across the country. Taxpayers who come into a service bureau can be shown by tax officials how to access the required information and services online.

This one-to-one education enables taxpayers to access services online and reduces the need for future visits to service bureaus.

- Informing taxpayers via media, information leaflets and electronic channels increases awareness and makes it easier for them to comply. The ETCB emphasises reciprocal partnerships and co-operation with taxpayers, supported by efficient information systems which provide relevant and timely information.

Apart from the media, the ETCB's work is promoted by other state and city institutions, including the Estonian Chamber of Commerce and Industry, the Estonian Association of Small and Medium Enterprises, the taxpayers association, and at community events and fairs.

Focus on: e-Tax/e-Customs Initiative

All of the ETCB's services are now available on its e-Tax/e-Customs Internet site (Box 10.3). Access to the e-Tax/e-Customs system is free and widely available to the public. This portal was launched in 2000 to enable secure exchanges of information between taxpayers and the tax administration. Today, the system offers around 30 electronic services for individual taxpayers and 70 services for business taxpayers (Box 10.2). For example, customs declarations and notices can be submitted electronically, and taxpayers can monitor in real time their tax accounting, tax liabilities and payments, as well as communicate with the ETCB securely.

Box 10.2. Using technology to make life easier for taxpayers and officials alike

- Business clients can access the ETCB website (www.emta.ee/eparingud) on their Smartphones or other smart devices to check tax-related information such as their tax debt, their Estonian value-added tax (VAT) registration number and their personal reference number for payments. In the future, this capability will be expanded to allow the ETCB to message taxpayers through their smart devices.
- New communication methods and systems are making contact with taxpayers more efficient. For example, every ETCB Service Bureau is now equipped with a Skype videophone, and a Customer Relationship Management (CRM) system registers face-to-face contacts, phone calls and e-letters from taxpayers. The information is used to understand reasons for contact so as to improve products and services generally, but also to record important information about individual taxpayers to improve communication (for example, language and communication channel preference).
- Every taxpayer generally has only one prepayment account and a single reference number in the ETCB system. This makes it easier for taxpayers to pay their tax, regardless of the type of tax due and the due date.

Source: Estonian Tax and Customs Board.

The ETCB is constantly improving the services provided by e-Tax/e-Customs. Since May 2013, every user can easily generate his/her own online certificate of absence of tax arrears or statement of balance. Using a digital stamp they can validate the certificate and send it as an official document by e-mail to others.

Figure 10.1. **Number of taxpayers using service bureaus in Estonia has decreased**

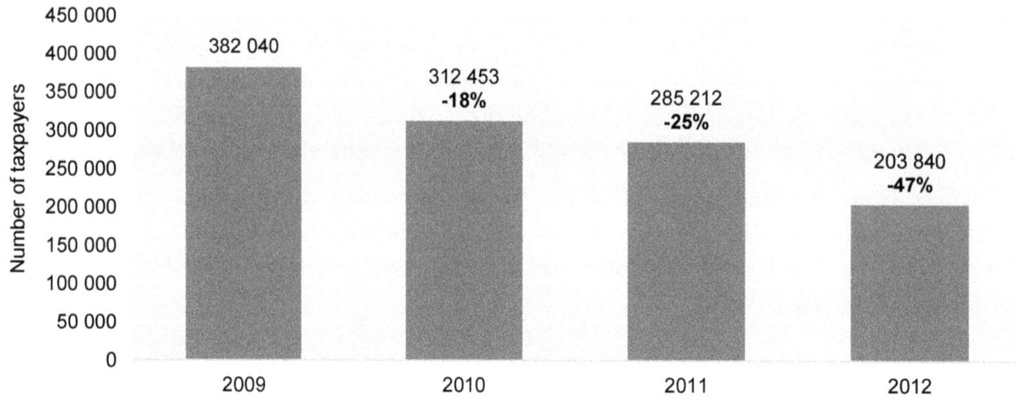

Source: Estonian Tax and Customs Board.

As of June 2013, e-Tax/e-Customs has linked with a new internal system called IRIS (named after the mythological Greek messenger goddess). IRIS sends taxpayers notifications of approaching due dates for filing tax returns or tax payments owed via automatically generated e-mail and SMS messages. Taxpayers can log into e-Tax/e-Customs to view their notifications and complete the necessary returns or make payments.

Previously, business access to e-Tax/e-Customs services was only possible by physically signing a contract at the ETCB's Service Bureau. Now contracts can be concluded electronically by a company representative, with the possibility of granting limited access to company employees for specific services in e-Tax/e-Customs.

Any new electronic services are introduced as clearly as possible to taxpayers, building on their familiarity with the e-Tax/e-Customs interface (which has been around for 13 years). For example, IRIS was launched through a press release informing taxpayers about the new system and its aim of making tax formalities simpler.

ETCB staff receive continuous training, such as specific training in new electronic systems like IRIS. Staff were also intensively involved in the testing phase of the system.

There are 73 employees in total working on e-Tax/e-Customs: 12 in the Service Department, 53 in the Tax Department and 8 in the Revenue Department.

Impacts

The ETCB's efforts to simplify taxpaying have resulted in improvements across a range of indicators:

- increased taxpayer satisfaction
- an increase in the number of clients who are using online self-service channels
- a decrease in visits by taxpayers to service bureaus (Figure 10.1)
- an increase in the voluntary compliance rate
- a decrease in the amount of tax debt.

Lessons learnt

The ECTB is preparing further improvements to its systems. A project to simplify the language used in administrative acts, notifications and other texts is planned, as well as an updated online self-service channel (compatible with mobile and other smart devices), and expanding the use of electronic documents.

Box 10.3. The Estonian Tax and Customs Board (ETCB)

The ETCB's mission is to collect the state's tax revenue, to protect Estonia's society and economy, and to improve the business environment.

The ETCB's 1 545 staff, organised into 16 service bureaus and 10 customs border-crossing points, aim to fulfil this mission by:

- making fulfilling tax obligations simple and quick – service quality is constantly being improved with increasing use of innovative channels of communication with taxpayers
- providing clients with timely information – new ways of informing taxpayers are being developed which are in a simple and easily understandable language
- making the service processes faster and more effective – replacing routine manual labour with fast data collection and analysis.

For more information:

Website: www.emta.ee

e-Tax/e-Customs Internet site: www.emta.ee/index.php?id=29761

Source: Estonian Tax and Customs Board.

Chapter 11

Guatemala: When it comes to taxes, strength lies in numbers

Superintendence for Tax Administration

This chapter presents Guatemala's taxpayer education programme. It first gives an overview of the whole programme and its objectives, followed by a focus on one specific element, the Citizen Culture Festival "Strength Lies in Numbers". It finally looks at the impacts and lessons learnt of the initiative.

Tax education in Guatemala aims to encourage constructive values and a positive attitude towards citizen tax contribution. It recognises that the best promoter of tax education is well-managed, efficient, rational and transparent public expenditures. It pursues inclusive and participatory activities – an approach which is culturally suited to Guatemala's social context.

Guatemala's Permanent Tax Culture Programme (PTCP) builds popular awareness of the importance of tax for the country's economic and social progress. This programme was created in 2005 by the Superintendence for Tax Administration (*Superintendencia de Administración Tributaria* or SAT; Box 11.3) with the aim of encouraging voluntary compliance with tax obligations.

Training in tax awareness is part of the broader process of constructing good citizenship. The programme has been working closely with other institutions with similar interests in civic training, the rights of children and adolescents, education in civic values and the promotion of responsible citizenship in general (Box 11.1).

Guatemala's taxpayer education

Since 2007, taxpayer education in Guatemala has been the responsibility of the Tax Culture Department. The programme is managed by a co-ordinator who brings together the department's three areas of work – education, information and promotion. Each of these is the responsibility of one of three specialised advisors, backed up by full-time and part-time staff.

Box 11.1. Objectives of Guatemala's taxpayer education

- Explain the importance of paying tax for the country's economic and social progress.
- Encourage values and attitudes that are consistent with a developing tax culture.
- Position tax culture as one of the fundamental pillars of the country's modernisation and development.

Source: Superintendence for Tax Administration.

With the inclusion of tax culture as a subject in the Basic National Syllabus (CNB), the programme is particularly active in schools, providing educational material such as school books and board games for primary school students, audiovisual tutorials, and teaching guides for Basic Cycle education and seminars on tax issues for graduating students. These are supported by the "Top Score in Tax Culture" Programme which aims to achieve full use of tax culture material and actions by all schools in target municipalities.

Other educational initiatives include a Mayan-language training programme for rural communities and a virtual tax review course for accounting experts.

Key promotion activities include:

- tax lotteries (to promote awareness of paying VAT; involves depositing official receipts to win prizes)
- citizen culture festivals, such as "Strength Lies in Numbers" (see below)

- a programme to build a culture of compliance with customs rules
- the *Municipio Cabal* Project.

Box 11.2. "*Municipio Cabal*" Project

Through its "*Municipio Cabal*" Project, the SAT partners with local governments across the country to promote a culture of full compliance at the local level through co-operative actions to improve transparency and accountability on the part of government and encourage social participation and ethical behaviour on the part of citizens.

For more information, see: http://eurosocialfiscal.org/uploads/media/Otra/folleto_SAT.pdf (in Spanish).

Source: Superintendence for Tax Administration.

Along with the production and distribution of many different products for tax information, training and awareness, the programme also invests heavily in the media with several written press publications, advertisements on national and local radio stations, and television broadcasts. It also has a website and a presence on social networks.

Another initiative is the production of "tax dramas" based on a story about a character named Simón – an honest and enterprising citizen as well as a good taxpayer committed to his family and country. These are aired on television and YouTube, and at public activities.

The programme works closely with the Ministries of Education and Finance and municipalities, the National Association of Municipalities, the *Instituto de Fomento Municipal*, the German Development Co-operation (GIZ) agency, the *Proyecto Educativo Pantaleón*, the International Plan, the *Centro Educativo Benito Juárez*, the *Colegio Naleb'* and Share Guatemala.

Focus on: The Citizen Culture Festival: "Strength Lies in Numbers"

"Strength Lies in Numbers" is a festival organised every year by the SAT to promote positive tax culture and citizenship among different partner institutions and target groups. The first such festival was held in April 2008. The title has been used for all subsequent festivals, with four festivals having taken place so far. The first festivals took place in the capital, Guatemala City, while the most recent festivals were held in the towns of Quetzaltenango and Cobán.

The social value of these citizenship culture festivals is clear: they include many artistic and cultural events, such as during the opening and closing ceremonies, as well as displays of artistic talent. Many families came to the closing day of the first festival, visiting exhibitions in the *Sector Cuatro Grados Norte* area of Guatemala City. The second festival ended with a concert, and the closing ceremonies of the third and fourth festivals involved public celebrations in the towns' main squares.

As children are one of the programme's priority target groups, many activities during the festivals have been designed to involve them. These include:

- the opening ceremonies

- the audiovisual work "El Hacedor de LLuvia" (The Rainmaker), an ancient Mayan legend which illustrates the importance of individual contribution to the common good
- guided visits under the "Get to Know Your City" educational programme
- the premiere of the TV series *Micos y Pericos*, using puppets to teach children about tax and citizenship issues
- the Good Citizen Rally with play areas set up by various participating organisations to teach tax culture and citizenship through play, covering topics such as environmental protection, traffic regulations, children's rights, consumer rights and the importance of saving money
- a working breakfast at the National Palace with members of the cabinet and other senior public officials
- "Superintendent and Intendants [Public Official] for a Day," where children share a workday with the SAT's Superintendent and five officials
- "Examples of Our Children's Artistic Talent," at the Municipal Theatre of Quetzaltenango along with various artistic groups.

Other festival activities were designed to engage teenagers, another priority target of the programme:

- a closing concert on the theme of "Strength Lies in Numbers," which involves thousands of teenagers
- an awards ceremony and musical show
- an indoor football tournament held on the sports fields of Quetzaltenango
- a "Contribution Mural" on the front wall of the *Centro de Estudios Tributarios* (SAT) in Guatemala City, painted by hundreds of young student graduates
- the Student Talent Show held in Quetzaltenango by groups of young artists in front of a large young audience
- an exhibition in Cobán on "Examples of Our Adolescents' Artistic Talent"
- an inspiring conference for teenagers, presented by the mountain climber Andrea Cardona entitled "Reaching Our Own Everest".

Apart from schools, universities and research centres have also participated in the citizen culture festivals. Key events included a presentation of a digital version of a study by the *Instituto Centroamericano de Estudios Fiscales* (ICEFI) entitled "History of Taxation in Guatemala", and various forums on subjects ranging from "The Role of the Press in Citizenship Training" and "Citizenship and National Identity", to "The Role of Taxation in Municipal Strengthening" and "Taxation Psychology".

The festivals mobilised a team of eight to ten people on-site, and six field workers. Other members of the SAT's staff, from all hierarchical levels, were involved. The Tax Culture Co-ordinator was in charge of the initiative, including overall organisation and inter-institutional relations. The managers of the education, information and promotion areas organised activities specific to their areas, and the Deputy Manager was responsible for administration and finance.

Many of the events were held jointly with other institutions, which also provided resources and staff. Other activities – such as the concert and show organisation, and citizen training – were outsourced to qualified external suppliers.

Each festival costs an average of USD 75 000, mostly for communication and promotion. Outsourcing to external suppliers costs approximately USD 25 000 on average for each festival. Third-party contributions have varied, for example: hiring premises, logistical support, transport and meals for school groups, announcements and transfers, and sponsorship of children participating in the "Superintendent and Intendants for a Day" events.

Impacts

Although this initiative has not been formally measured or assessed, it has successfully achieved the aim of encouraging popular awareness of tax issues. Table 11.1 shows the attendance at these events over the years. The lower numbers for the 2010 and 2011 festivals reflect the move from the capital Guatemala City to the smaller regional centres of Quetzaltenango and Cobán.

Table 11.1. **Participation in citizen culture festivals in Guatemala, 2008-10**

	Number of participants				
Year	Institutional and academic events	Children's events	Adolescent events	Events for all ages	Total
2008	850	4 300	2 800	3 500	11 450
2009	475	3 100	1 700	2 000	7 275
2010	550	2 600	2 400	1 500	7 050
2011	450	2 600	1 600	1 000	5 650
Total	2 325	12 600	8 500	8 000	31 425

Source: Tax Culture, SAT.

They have enabled the SAT to project a new, more positive image not only to those directly involved in the events, but also to the general public through extensive media coverage. Diana Freire, Manager of the *Centro de Estudios Tributarios*, considers that the festivals have been very effective in bringing the tax administration closer to society, children, adolescents and Guatemalan families in general. She has pointed out that apart from encouraging tax awareness, these activities "touch participant emotions, leaving behind a greater legacy than any other on-site training programme".

Lessons learnt

High-level political support raises the profile of the events and reinforces the importance of the messages. Festivals have been opened by the President, the Vice President and the Minister of Finance. Such representation in turn helps to attract other significant speakers, including a former mayor of Bogotá and candidate to the Presidency of Colombia; the UN Special Rapporteur on the promotion and protection of the right to freedom of opinion and expression, the Executive Secretary of the Inter-American Center of Tax Administrations (CIAT) and the Mexican Ambassador in Guatemala.

The citizen culture festivals have shown that new forms of co-operation with other organisations, such as private companies and the academic sector, can be valuable in promoting good citizenship.

It is important that the tax administration makes the most of these new opportunities by, for example, building on these new inter-institutional relations and fully assessing the festivals' impact on target groups. Permanent recreational-educational areas are of great interest, giving the SAT the opportunity to manage all the information and training needs of students and teachers in tax culture matters. Likewise, citizen training visits are a promising way forward for both the SAT and partner organisations. In the future, a joint educational programme for various institutions could be considered, perhaps to create a permanent exhibition centre that covers all taxation issues: taxes, customs, foreign trade, social security, central banking and financial supervision.

Box 11.3. The Superintendence for Tax Administration

The Superintendence for Tax Administration (SAT) was created on 21 February 1998 by a state decree. Its aims are to administer tax and customs in a modern, efficient and effective manner, thereby increasing tax revenues with sustainability, honesty and transparency.

The SAT is a decentralised institution with full functional, economic, financial, technical and administrative autonomy. It has a total of 4 000 employees, and covers Guatemala's 4 regions and 22 departments. Its headquarters are located in Guatemala City.

For more information:

Website: www.sat.gob.gt

Tax Culture website: http://portal.sat.gob.gt/ct/portal

Taxpayer education e-mail address: culturatributaria@sat.gob.gt

Source: Superintendence for Tax Administration.

Chapter 12

Jamaica: STEP – The Schools Taxpayer Education Programme

Jamaica Tax Administration

This chapter presents Jamaica's taxpayer education programme. It first gives an overview of the whole programme and its objectives, followed by a focus on one specific element, the Schools Taxpayer Education Programme (STEP). An additional section provides information on the staffing and costs of STEP. It subsequently looks at the impacts and lessons learnt of the initiative, followed by an outlook on next steps.

Tax Administration Jamaica (TAJ; see Box 12.3) was created in 2011 by bringing together the former Inland Revenue Department, Taxpayer Audit and Assessment and the Tax Administration Services Departments. With this came a much-needed refocusing and restructuring of Jamaica's taxpayer education programme: today there are education teams in the seven main regional areas, covering the entire island.

Jamaica's taxpayer education

The TAJ has a comprehensive mix of communications and public relations strategies aimed at a large cross-section of the population: from students to senior citizens, informal traders and professional associations, personal and corporate taxpayers, as well as the property, motor and religious sectors.

Box 12.1. **Objectives of Jamaica's taxpayer education**

- Improve and promote voluntary compliance with registering, filing, reporting and paying tax.
- Promote a positive view of tax and increase tax literacy, thereby increasing the number of contributing citizens.
- Build a culture of tax compliance among the nation's youth.
- Show citizens how to pay taxes.
- Explain why taxes should be paid.
- Empower citizens to engage in discussions on the use of tax revenue.

Source:Jamaica Tax Administration.

The programme draws substantially on a media presence to achieve its objectives (Box 12.1), using both traditional and non-traditional media platforms. Advertising and news releases are primarily through national and community radio, television and newspapers, with advertising being particularly prevalent around major tax dates and the introduction of new measures and service options. On a more regular basis are weekly radio series on several stations offering tax tips, as well as a companion weekly and monthly print series published in a major national newspaper. Other print media includes brochures, flyers, posters and booklets.

Non-traditional media such as social media (Facebook and Twitter), the TAJ website, online advertising and digital media boards/screens in tax offices are more widely used to reach a younger, more technologically savvy audience, both nationally and internationally. The dynamic and interactive nature of these allows for up-to-date information on a wide range of tax issues as well as access to the Jamaica Tax Portal, through which tax returns can be filed and payments made. The TAJ website also provides an interface with Twitter. The URL is accessible through direct links with other related government and business association websites, such as the critical Institute of Chartered Accountants of Jamaica.

Seminars and workshops; community and cultural events; contests, awards and exhibitions also serve to build awareness among the general public, whilst the more specialised School's Taxpayer Education Programme (STEP) targets higher education institutions, secondary schools and elementary schools. These are all facilitated by taxpayer education teams at the revenue service centres (the main tax offices). There is also a care centre: a central toll-free service through which the public can get information and guidance on a wide range of tax issues and service options. The care centre also provides a courtesy call service to customers reminding them of due dates and promotes available service options.

In general, the TAJ has had tremendous success engaging and partnering with other institutions and organisations, making it possible to develop, implement and expand its programmes to meet the particular needs of various stakeholders. At a public level, this involves government departments and agencies, schools and universities. The TAJ has also established a strong relationship with the media via a spokesperson who participates in public interviews and discussion programmes on a regular basis. Other areas of partnering include civil society, business organisations, the Institute of Chartered Accountants of Jamaica, the Caribbean Organisation of Tax Administrators and the Jamaica Business Development Company.

Focus on: Schools Taxpayer Education Programme

The idea of a STEP initially came about in the late 1990s in Jamaica's former Income Tax Department, the aim being to foster a culture of voluntary compliance and to highlight the role and purpose of paying taxes. The programme was introduced on a small scale, with a single officer responsible for assisting secondary school students in grades 10, 11 and 12. It was focused on income tax.

Over the years the programme has expanded to cater to students at the tertiary level, and to focus on all tax types. From the early 2000s the programme was carried out by two tax departments. However, further expansion of the programme was unfortunately stymied by limited financial and human resources.

Following the 2011 emergence of the TAJ, the programme was reconfigured, expanded and re-launched in 2012 and increased the emphasis on voluntary compliance. It was agreed that it was important to address not just secondary and tertiary education, but also to introduce the STEP in primary schools. The relaunched programme exposes students to taxpayers' rights and responsibilities under Jamaican tax laws, as well as to the benefits of paying taxes (particularly in the work and business environment). In doing this, the programme seeks to get students to positively influence the attitudes of their parents/guardians and other adults with whom they interact. Through the STEP, the nation's youth become agents of change, raising the tax literacy of the country and creating a future in which paying taxes is seen as a vital civic duty. At the primary level the purpose is to generate overall excitement about tax. The programme also aims to develop an understanding among students in grades three to six about how goods and services are funded by the government and to explain why it is important for everyone to contribute by paying tax.

In secondary and tertiary education, the main objective is to equip and prepare students for the workplace, as well as to expose them to the different career options available at the TAJ.

The STEP engages with a mix of techniques and media channels to reach a wide cross-section of schools and students, using traditional, social and digital media to interface with students at all levels and to reach a younger, tech-savvy generation. It also works with the Ministry of Education to officially notify schools engaged with the STEP of any competitions being held by the TAJ (Box 12.2).

Box 12.2. Competitions for school children

A school essay competition is held twice a year under the umbrella of the STEP to coincide with the regional competition staged by the Caribbean Organisation of Tax Administrators (COTA). This engages secondary students to research and write on identified tax subjects, with the possibility of an award.

Source:Jamaica Tax Administration.

The STEP is multifaceted and can be customised to suit each target group, with different delivery methodologies employed according to the age and grade levels of the students. In primary schools there is a more interactive approach, using a specially created puzzle booklet and a short video called "Why Tax". Different methodologies also enable students to be creative, as they are encouraged to develop tax jingles/poems, etc.

In secondary and tertiary education, PowerPoint presentations help to keep students fully engaged. These focus on the role of tax administration, the types of taxes and why taxes are necessary and also include case studies and group tasks. Publications, such as a "School Leavers" brochure, are circulated as reference material available to take home. Career expos and large-scale seminars are also organised, particularly for secondary schools, to target a large number of students on the principles of tax and tax career opportunities.

The programme is promoted through advertising on national radio, via social media and in newspapers. It is also promoted in national student newspaper publications as well as in direct mailings to schools by the Ministry of Education. Moreover, a STEP sign-up form is available on its website, through which schools may sign-up to invite resource persons to visit and deliver the programme.

In general, this programme is delivered by the taxpayer education teams within the formal school system. The TAJ also has developed some fruitful partnerships which have extended the STEP's reach considerably.

For example, the TAJ's recent partnership with Junior Achievement Jamaica (JAJ) and the Ministry of Education has allowed the TAJ to expand the STEP considerably to reach more students in a structured way. The JAJ already has an established primary school programme, so the TAJ/JAJ partnership has meant that the STEP has been available at the primary level across the entire island since September 2012.

At the secondary level, the TAJ/JAJ partnership has also allowed the programme to expand so that students who have an interest in business can engage directly with the TAJ. In 2013, the TAJ participated in the JAJ webinar and conference which involved students from over 30 schools. The TAJ was able to interact and share information with these students; a number of them took the opportunity to apply for their taxpayer registration number (TRN) and received guidance on tax relevant to business.

In previous years there was a partnership with a leading radio station, Radio Jamaica. Their "School's Out" series involve special broadcasts from different schools. Participating in these events allowed the TAJ to teach tax to a much larger audience, not only the students from the schools at which the event was being held, but also thousands of other students who tuned in at these times.

A partnership with the government agency Jamaica Business Development Corporation helps to bolster the STEP tertiary level programme, as it enables the STEP to interface with undergraduates pursuing entrepreneurial studies. Through this partnership potential entrepreneurs and future industry leaders are exposed to the principles of being a good corporate citizen and a responsible taxpayer. They get a hands-on look at applying tax principles such as tax registration, tax filing and how to pay tax, as well as the rights and responsibilities of a taxpayer.

Staffing and costs of the programme

The initiative involves 24 employees in total, divided into teams of 3 or 4 at each of the 7 regional offices. The TAJ team members are given training prior to each phased enhancement of the programme.

There is a specific budget allocated for taxpayer service/education initiatives from which funds are earmarked for the STEP. These funds are limited and are mostly used for printing brochures, activity booklets and the TAJ branded pencils. Savings have been made by digitalising material and using erasable, re-usable foam presentation boards. Advertising is minimal and low-cost ways of promoting the STEP are sought out to keep costs to a minimum.

Impacts

The initiative has not been externally evaluated, but its success is judged by the number of schools and students it is reaching.

- An increasing number of young people are being reached. Between 1 April 2012 and 31 March 2013, a total of 123 schools were visited, reaching 11 166 students. Between 1 April 2013 and 31 May 2013, the programme had already visited 26 schools, involving a target group of 2 024 students.
- Greater awareness. There has been a great increase in awareness and knowledge among future taxpayers; more students are now applying to work at the TAJ to become part of a movement to influence the business world. With the increased awareness of the programme there has also been an increase in the number of schools inviting taxpayer education teams to come in and address their students.
- More positive attitudes. A healthier, more positive attitude has developed among this demographic. There is also a general feeling that the government is spending taxes wisely and that the tax administration is one where the taxpayer is treated fairly and transparently. Students now have a better understanding of how the TAJ's work is in the interest of the country and are able to see the importance of paying taxes.
- Better tax compliance. The overall tax compliance of this group has somewhat improved in the past five years and – more dramatically – the moral obligation to pay taxes "voluntarily" has been greatly strengthened.

The TAJ has received a verbal recommendation from school principals, as well as from the Chairmen of Junior Achievement Jamaica and the CEO of the Jamaica Business Development Corporation. Furthermore, the TAJ was asked to share its model of

Taxpayer Education and Communications with the Caribbean tax partners at the Caribbean Organisation of Tax Administrators Conference in 2012.

Lessons learnt

Having a dedicated team responsible for implementing taxpayer education has been critical to the success of the STEP. Partnerships have also been crucial, allowing the STEP to expand its reach significantly.

The key challenge has been the lack of funds for printing publications. With more funding the programme could print more publications and procure professionally developed instructional and promotional video items. The idea would be to use these as give-aways to students who display the greatest interest and creativity during sessions.

Next steps

Ideas for enhancing the programme include running a taxation jingle competition. The winning jingle would then be professionally produced. Greater impact could be achieved by working with the Ministry of Education to incorporate tax matters into the formal primary and secondary curricula. This would form part of a social studies programme or civics course.

Box 12.3. Tax Administration Jamaica (TAJ)

The TAJ was established on 1 April 2011, under the Revenue Administration (Amendment) Act 2011. Its primary goal is to foster voluntary tax compliance, collect revenue in an equitable and efficient manner, contribute to a competitive business environment and facilitate economic growth and development. The programme is carried out by approximately 2 500 staff, distributed across 30 revenue centres and tax offices.

As the main tax administration body, the TAJ is responsible not only for implementing tax laws and regulations, but also for providing property management services for tax offices and revenue service centres. It is also responsible for processing drivers' licences and managing the motor vehicle registry.

For more information:

Website: www.jamaicatax.gov.jm

Email: taxhelp@taj.gov.jm

Source:Jamaica Tax Administration.

Chapter 13

Kenya: The Schools Outreach Programme

Kenya Revenue Authority (KRA)

This chapter presents Kenya's taxpayer education programme. It first gives an overview of the whole programme and its objectives, followed by a focus on one specific element, the Schools Outreach Programme. It finally looks at the impacts and lessons learnt of the initiative.

The Kenya Revenue Authority (KRA, see Box 13.2) is a government agency that aims to run its operations in the same way as a well-functioning, efficient private enterprise. In order to offer better single-window services to taxpayers, the KRA is divided into five regions (Rift Valley, Western, Southern, Northern and Central).

Kenya's taxpayer education

Recognising the need to educate both existing and potential taxpayers, the KRA established a special unit for taxpayer education in 2005: the Taxpayer Education Unit (TEU). The TEU is one of four core units within the Large Taxpayers office service chain. It is currently staffed by three full-time officers, but is complemented by officers from other sections as needs arise (Box 13.1).

Box 13.1. **Objectives of taxpayer education in Kenya**

- Promote a culture of tax understanding, engagement and compliance amongst Kenya's citizens.
- Explain why and how taxes should be paid.
- Increase tax literacy.
- Empower citizens to engage in discussions on the use of tax revenue.

Source: Kenya Revenue Authority (KRA).

Key tax messages are communicated through:

- the use of national television, though only for special activities and issues due to the high costs involved
- the use of local vernacular stations – they have wide outreach and are cost effective
- the use of national and regional newspapers
- mobile tax services and visits to public institutions and services outside of urban centres by KRA officers to reach taxpayers in areas without tax offices
- seminars and workshops, contests and awards as well as community and cultural events for taxpayers and potential taxpayers, such as students in higher education institutions or secondary schools
- the extensive use of pamphlets, booklets and flyers in English and the local language, Kiswahili.
- the KRA works with the media (for advertising and news), other state institutions (in particular the Ministry of Education) and professional organisations such as the Kenya Association of Manufacturers, the United Business Association, the Kenya International Freight Forwarders Association and the Kenya National Chamber of Commerce and Industry.

Focus on: Schools Outreach Programme

The School Outreach Programme is a long-term programme, launched in 2012 by the TEU. Its purpose is to promote a taxpaying culture among future taxpayers. Students are taught the origins and history of taxation, and the importance of taxation in the economy and daily life. The ultimate goal is for them to act as tax "ambassadors".

One of the programme's core elements is the establishment of tax clubs in schools where students can discuss tax issues. The TEU sets up the tax clubs and supports them by providing guides to run these clubs and organising regional and national activities in which tax clubs are invited to participate.

In 2013, a national competition was to be organised by the TEU for tax clubs. This competition was planned to take place at the end of the year and was to be funded directly by the KRA as there is no external support. The competition involves a debate between different school clubs on taxation themes. A panel of judges comprising teachers and tax experts were to decide the winning teams.

Beyond this, the TEU also conducts school visits and gives short lectures on taxation for students. Seminars for school teachers are also held to enhance teacher knowledge of taxation issues. Reading and promotional materials are produced and distributed.

Twenty employees are involved in the programme, though not on a full-time basis: four working at the national level, ten at the regional level and six at the local level. This was insufficient given the scope and size of such a project, so other officers from sister units and sections have been brought in to roll out the programme.

Staff training takes place over a period of two days and provides an overview of Kenya's tax system, its benefits and the importance of compliance. Capacity building in the regional offices allows other officers to be able to run the programmes on behalf of the KRA.

The total cost of the initiative for 2013/14 amounted to KES 20 million (USD 231 000). Of course, more funding would be welcome; the project has received no external funding.

Impact

Post-lecture evaluations on the level of satisfaction indicate positive results from students, teachers and the school administrations. However, as the programme has begun to target future taxpayers and hence has a long-term perspective, measurable impacts on tax compliance are not instantly visible.

- Taxpayers reached. To date, over 25 000 students and 400 teachers have been reached by the School Outreach Programme, resulting in greater tax awareness among targeted groups as well as an enhanced sense of moral obligation to pay taxes voluntarily.
- Attitudes changed. The issues around taxes have been seen to be demystified and a positive attitude has been noted among the participants. A general lack of awareness of tax issues has been supplanted by a positive recognition and appreciation of the benefits of taxation and of compliance. This has improved perceptions that taxpayers are treated fairly and transparently by the tax administration. However, there has been only a slight increase in taxpayers feeling that the government spends their tax money wisely, and that the overall tax burden is fairly distributed amongst taxpayers.

- Demand generated. The post-lecture evaluations indicate that students, teachers and the school administrations are satisfied with the initiative, with demand for more information and follow-up activities.

Lessons learnt

The main challenges for the initiative are the lack of human and financial resources. There are only two officers in charge of the outreach programme, and they also handle other activities within the TEU. This understaffing is a significant challenge as there is a serious lack of programme developers and trainers. The budget for the outreach programme comes from the small TEU budget, and although increased funding for the programme has been sought, low budget allocation generally means that the programme is unlikely to be implemented as fully as anticipated. Therefore, new internal and external partners need to be found. Internal staffing procedures have helped resolve some of these challenges.

There is high demand for this programme in Kenya, and several ideas on how it could develop: for example, teacher training could be expanded to establish a network of "agents for change". An open web portal could become a resource point for teachers and students that would greatly enhance the project.

Other ideas for improving the current programmes include integrating taxpayer education into the school curriculum, additional mobile taxpayer units and specific programmes for universities and colleges.

Box 13.2. The Kenya Revenue Authority (KRA)

Founded in 1995, the KRA is responsible for collecting revenue on behalf of the government of Kenya. The Ministry of Finance sets policy to guide the KRA's operations. The KRA's mission is "to promote compliance with Kenya's tax, trade, and border legislation and regulation by promoting the standards set out in the Taxpayers Charter and responsible enforcement by highly motivated and professional staff thereby maximi[s]ing revenue collection at the least possible cost for the socio-economic well-being of Kenyans." Its vision is "To be the leading Revenue Authority in the world, respected for professionalism integrity and fairness". Its strategic theme is "attaining international best practice in revenue administration by investing in a professional team, deepening reforms and quality service delivery to enhance compliance."

The KRA has 4 500 employees and 65 offices across Kenya, and reports directly to the Ministry of Finance.

For more information:

Website: www.kra.go.ke

Taxpayer education e-mail address: callcentre@kra.go.ke

Source: Kenya Revenue Authority (KRA).

Chapter 14

Korea: Tax classes for small businesses

National Tax Service

This chapter presents Korea's taxpayer education programme. It first gives an overview of the whole programme and its objectives, followed by a focus on one specific element, the tax classes for business. It finally looks at the impacts of the initiative.

The National Tax Service (NTS; see Box 14.3) is Korea's main tax administration body. Since 2001 it has been working hard to create some consistency among its various service channels. Previously, these were scattered throughout the organisation – from district tax offices, regional tax offices, to the main office – making it difficult for taxpayers to maintain consistent contact with the NTS. This, plus a lack of expertise, resulted in unsatisfactory service quality. Moreover, some tax officers, particularly in district tax offices, were frequently disrupted by telephone inquiries; an NTS call centre was established in 2001 to manage all tax-related inquiries.

In July 2008, the NTS set up an integrated management system to allow it to better respond to complaints and requests, thereby improving its service. The NTS also expanded the functions of the National Tax Consultation to create the Customer Satisfaction Centre which now handles all tax-related inquiries.

Korea's taxpayer education

There is no central taxpayer education unit in the NTS, so tax education activities are carried out internally by tax officers (Box 14.1). The National Tax Officials Training Institute (NTOTI), an affiliate of the NTS, is responsible for enhancing tax officers' expertise and also carries out some activities, including the taxpayer education programme described below.

Box 14.1. **Objectives of taxpayer education in Korea**

- Ensure just and fair tax practice by exposing Korea's underground economy.
- Provide support for taxpayers and in doing so, raise morale and attitudes about tax.
- Secure the revenue base.
- Expand support for taxpayers to revitalise the economy.
- Create a transparent, trustworthy administration.

Source: National Tax Service.

The NTS also provides education programmes to help taxpayers deal with tax matters, to encourage tax compliance and promote tax policies. These programmes differ according to the needs and type of audience:

- a TV talk show and comedy show highlight the daily difficulties NTS staff face in promoting tax compliance
- a Smartphone messenger service allows Smartphone users to access and add the NTS to their friend list so that they can receive regular updates
- SNS reporters: these consist of 30 persons from all walks of life (e.g. housewives, students, office workers, etc.) who talk about tax issues from their different perspectives
- the NTS Tax Museum has been renovated and refashioned to broaden and deepen students' understanding of taxes (www.nts.go.kr//museum//main.asp).

In addition to educating the nation, the NTS also encourages taxpayers through a number of other initiatives.

Exemplary taxpayers. The NTS has adopted this system to recognise and benefit exemplary taxpayers. This system applies to both Korean companies and foreign companies investing in Korea. A business taxpayer who meets certain requirements (Box 14.2) can be selected as an exemplary taxpayer by the Exemplary Taxpayer Review Committee. This status gives them the following benefits:

- exemption from having to provide collateral when taxes up to KRW 500 million are not paid immediately
- suspension of tax audits for up to three years
- reduced interest rates on loans
- discounted train fares and medical expenses for the taxpayer and his/her employees
- use of the VIP window at airport immigrations
- free parking at state-run public parking lots.

Box 14.2. **What makes an exemplary taxpayer?**

Taxpaying companies which are approved by Exemplary Taxpayer Review Committee must meet the following conditions:

- continuous operation of business for more than five years
- tax income in the black for three years running
- no disguised or fictitious data reported for three years running
- fairly large taxable income for three years running
- no unpaid or overdue taxes (including the representative's) in the past three years
- a tax audit which confirms no intentional tax evasion
- taxable income reported honestly compared to other taxpayers

Source: NTS Annual Report 2013, available at: http://www.nts.go.kr/eng/resources/resour_21.asp?minfoKey=MINF7420080211223143&type=V# (accessed 3 October 2013).

Source: National Tax Service.

E-books. The NTS publishes e-books which cover a range of tax-related queries and issues. These are uploaded onto the NTS website and are freely available to tax officers and taxpayers alike.

Cash Receipt Lottery (discontinued). The Cash Receipt Lottery used to be held monthly to encourage non-wage and salary earners who do not receive income deduction benefits (e.g. students) to request cash receipts. The lottery was drawn once a month on national TV with prize money ranging from KRW 50 000 (USD 50) for 5th place to KRW 100 million (USD 100 000) for 1st place.

Literature for young people. In 2008, the NTS published *Truths and Myths on Taxes for Teens* aimed at middle and high schools nationwide. The book looks at interesting tax-related facts and addresses some common tax-related questions, such as "Do we have to pay taxes on the money our parents give us on New Year's Day?"

Focus on: Tax classes for business

The NTS Taxpayer Education Programme was initiated to help individual and small-sized business taxpayers meet their tax obligations. It is run by the National Tax Officials Training Institute (NTOTI) and consists of 20 classes classified by tax types. The programme is open to everyone, and is easily accessible for all. Textbooks accompany the programme and are an additional resource, providing a clear understanding of tax matters. Local businesses are invited to take the classes at the six regional tax offices.

The NTS works hard to inform Korean businesses and individuals overseas of their tax options. In order to give the NTS support to small and medium-sized enterprises (SMEs) working overseas, lectures on international transaction regulations (or foreign tax information) are offered in big cities (e.g. Busan, Daejeon, etc.) where many companies trading overseas are headquartered. The NTS' public relations division sends regular, written notification to attendees by e-mail, informing them where and when lectures will take place. Further to this effort, regional tax offices notify the whereabouts and other information of events to the target SMEs by e-mail or phone.

For Korean companies or individuals living and doing business abroad, seminars are provided at local Korean embassies on matters such as capital gains tax, gift tax and offshore bank accounts. These have been held in Japan, the People's Republic of China and the United States for Korean residents or business taxpayers living there.

For the convenience of taxpayers living in rural or remote areas, lectures on VAT, corporate tax and capital gains tax are provided at local universities by NTOTI professors.

In terms of costs and staffing, on average two or three professors and one additional staff member are assigned to a single education programme. Approximately KRW 50 million (USD 50 000) is allotted to this programme every year.

Impacts

While there has been no external evaluation of these classes for businesses, the efforts to respond to taxpayers' needs, enhance programme quality and promote public relations have seen a steady increase in the number of programme participants and levels of satisfaction (Table 14.1).

Table 14.1. **Korea's expanding Tax Education Programme, 2010-12**

	2010	2011	2012	Total
Number of classes	42	56	58	156
Number of participants	6 151	7 248	8 262	21 651

Source: National Tax Service.

Through open conversations with programme participants, the NTS has gained a better sense of which tax matters need addressing, and these have been made more accessible to the taxpayer. Furthermore, valuable feedback from taxpayers is now passed up to NTS headquarters, where it can be incorporated into existing tax systems.

Box 14.3. National Tax Service (NTS)

The NTS is Korea's main tax body, with more than 20 000 tax officers nationwide, distributed across 12 bureaus, 6 regional tax offices and 111 district tax offices.

For more information:

- Website: www.nts.go.kr/eng
- Taxpayer education address: NTOTI, 1110-17, Gyeongsu-daero, Jangan-gu, Suwon-si, Gyeonggi-do, Republic of Korea, 440-290 (zip code)

Source: National Tax Service.

Chapter 15

Lebanon: The "Time for Taxes" calendar

Ministry of Finance

This chapter presents Lebanon's taxpayer education programme. It first gives an overview of the whole programme and its objectives, followed by a focus on one specific element, the "Time for Taxes" calendar. It finally looks at the impacts and lessons learnt of the initiative.

Lebanon's Ministry of Finance (MoF; Box 15.3) places great importance on broadening the tax base and improving tax compliance. It has focused its reform efforts on creating a modern and innovative tax administration by promoting taxpayer services and a tax culture that were virtually absent in Lebanon previously. Tax culture refers here to the means typically used to inform taxpayers, to the methods through which news and publications on taxation are disseminated and to the procedures enabling online access to tax services and information (Box 15.1). The MoF has launched a number of initiatives for informing and educating the public in order to promote voluntary compliance and create a new, enhanced image for the public administration.

Lebanon's taxpayer education

There is no dedicated unit for taxpayer education within the Ministry of Finance; instead it is mainstreamed throughout the various departments and directorates with responsibility for income tax, value-added tax (VAT), property tax, customs, etc.

Box 15.1. Objectives of taxpayer education in Lebanon

- Show citizens how to pay taxes.
- Increase the number of citizens who pay taxes.
- Increase citizens' tax literacy.

Source: Ministry of Finance, Lebanon.

Educational activities are many and varied. For example:

- To accompany the launch of new tax laws and institutional reforms (such as the introduction of the VAT, the establishment of the Large Taxpayers Office, the Deduction at Source for Salaries Department and the ratification of the Tax Procedures Code), the tax administration organises conferences, seminars and workshops for the public, professional groups, businessmen and trade associations. These are a chance for them to express their views and concerns and to explain new legislation, answer inquiries and clarify the implementation of new tax laws.
- Several guides, pamphlets and newsletters provide tax and fiscal information to citizens. Some are targeted to specific sectors.
- "Youth: Get to Know the Ministry of Finance" is a one-day orientation programme to introduce university students to the role and functions of the Ministry of Finance. The programme includes training on the Lebanese tax system.
- The MoF has an information centre to respond to taxpayers' email inquiries, as well as a 24/7 call centre. There is also a free downloadable application for mobile telephone users to inform them of deadlines for filing declarations and for payment, as well as the amount of tax due and updates.
- The MoF website has been revamped and transformed into a web portal to give citizens fast and easy access to economic, financial and fiscal information, news,

publications, notifications and e-services. In addition, a blog covering the activities of EU twinning projects was posted on the website.

- Massive media campaigns have been held to notify taxpayers of recently launched services. These include: *i)* TV advertisement campaigns aired on Lebanese stations to introduce the new LibanPost services (for paying the built property tax); *ii)* billboard and radio campaigns to introduce the call centre; *iii)* trilingual leaflets are distributed through major newspapers and magazines to promote new services and initiatives; and *iv)* a TV, unipoles, billboards and SMS campaign was recently launched aiming to increase shoppers' awareness about the importance of requesting an invoice with every purchase to discourage informal economic activity.
- Sonic branding has given the MoF a distinctive identity, and put it at the leading edge of the advertisement sector. A team of musicians created a unique jingle to make MoF audiovisual ads instantly recognisable everywhere. The new jingle is used by the call centre and in every MoF radio and TV campaign.
- A *Citizens' Budget* aims to increase transparency over public expenditure (Box 15.2)

Box 15.2. **Promoting transparency and accountability: The *Citizens' Budget***

The Ministry of Finance is collaborating with the Lebanese Transparency Association (LTA) to promote transparency and accountability. One such initiative is the *Citizens' Budget*, a non-technical document which allows citizens to inform themselves on public finance issues. It tracks major government expenditures, revenues and public debt in an effort to build citizens' knowledge on such information. It also serves as a tool to allow individuals and civil society groups to track the efficiency of public services as compared to the allocated funds. The document is developed following international best practices on transparency in public budgeting.

For more information, see the Lebanese Transparency Association webpage: www.transparency-lebanon.org/index.php?option=com_content&view=article&id=29&Itemid=59&lang=en (accessed 4 October 2103).

Source: Ministry of Finance, Lebanon.

In 2007, a taxpayer survey was conducted by a team of trained fieldworkers to assess, on the one hand, the impact of the MoF's awareness campaigns and on the other hand, taxpayers' satisfaction with the services provided. The questionnaire was designed by a research-oriented company and submitted to all stakeholders. The outcome of the survey helped improve services.

The MoF works closely with other government departments and agencies, as well as with LibanPost (Lebanon's postal service) for paying the built property tax. It also works with business organisations. The United Nations Development Programme's (UNDP) TA for Fiscal Management and Reform project (Tax Reform Team) is a key partner, working with the MoF to design and implement its reforms. These include merging the Revenue and the VAT Directorates, introducing risk management and integrating taxpayer education activities.

Focus on: The "Time for Taxes" desk calendar

Every year since 2006 the MoF has been sending out an annual "Time for Taxes" calendar along with the VAT declaration forms. The aim is to increase taxpayers' awareness of their rights and obligations, and to remind them of key submission dates. The calendar's content and design are updated every year. It is triangular-shaped so it can stand on a desk. There is one page for every month: one side of the page gives details about individual declarations, describing the tax obligation, the deadline for submission and the reference code for the form to be used by the taxpayer; the other side indicates the deadline for submitting declarations. On each page a brief "Did you know" section gives taxpayers various information on duties, rights, penalties, tips on how to use the ministry's website to access information, etc. There are also recommendations on what to do in an adversarial or exceptional case.

The tax calendar is a key tool for building citizens' tax literacy. The tax calendar is aimed at companies with an annual turnover above LBP 150 million (USD 100 000). In 2013, 30 000 copies of the 2013 tax calendar, in Arabic, were produced and distributed.

This project has been supported by the UNDP. It involves a team of ten employees at the national level. The total costs are approximately USD 70 000 and are funded entirely by the allocated operating budget.

Impacts

The impact of the initiative has been evaluated by the decrease of the number of late contributions.

- Greater reach. The calendar reaches approximately 30 000 taxpayers every year.
- Improvements in tax reporting. The calendar has helped taxpayers to meet important deadlines, especially for the VAT. It has increased the number of taxpayers and the tax yield and is therefore considered a success.
- More positive perceptions and greater tax literacy. The initiative has significantly increased people's sense of moral obligation to pay taxes "voluntarily". Furthermore, it has greatly improved taxpayers' knowledge of how to pay taxes. This is because forms are handed out with the tax calendar, which explains which form to use for which specific deadlines.

The initiative has also improved perceptions that other taxpayers are paying their fair share, helping to raise opinions of the tax administration itself.

Lessons learnt

There were no major problems encountered during the implementation of the initiative. There are no plans to increase the scope of the initiative, but it could be supplemented by other related taxpayer education activities.

Box 15.3. Lebanon's Ministry of Finance (MoF)

The MoF's vision is to lead the government's economic reform through the sound formulation and management of fiscal policy and public debt. The goal is to foster sustainable economic growth in alignment with national priorities, and act as a role model for transparency and accountability in a manner that reflects good governance.

The MoF's responsibilities include:

- ensure that the legal responsibilities of the ministry are impartially executed
- develop and maintain a stable economic environment
- structure optimally and manage the nation's assets and liabilities
- foster stable financial institutions and markets
- facilitate the development of the national economy and international trade
- communicate clearly the degree to which national spending is aligned with national objectives and priorities
- provide employees with the skills and resources required to effectively perform their responsibilities and to provide them with opportunities for career development and advancement
- facilitate co-operation among public agencies through finance
- develop and maintain leading edge organisational and management practices
- combat fraud and corruption within public finance and the financial system
- provide valuable, effective, friendly customer services to the public and private sectors.

For more information:

- Website: www.finance.gov.lb; www.finance.gov.lb/ar-LB/taxation/Pages/default.aspx; www.customs.gov.lb/customs/about/about.asp?id=2
- Taxpayer education e-mail address: infocenter@finance.gov.lb

Source: Ministry of Finance, Lebanon.

Chapter 16

Malaysia: Tax fun for children

Inland Revenue Board of Malaysia

This chapter presents Malaysia's taxpayer education programme. It first gives an overview of the whole programme and its objectives, followed by a focus on one specific element, the tax fun for children activities. It finally looks at the impacts of the initiative.

With its motto of "Together we develop the nation", the Inland Revenue Board of Malaysia (IRBM; Box 16.4) is continuously identifying and implementing new ways to make it easier for taxpayers to fulfil their tax obligations and understand the Malaysian tax system. As the tax arm of the government, the IRBM is successfully collecting revenues for reinvestment in infrastructure and education for the benefit of future generations.

Taxpayer education is carried out at headquarters and all branches, with a designated Taxpayer Education Division situated within the Corporate Services Department, overseen by the Chief Executive Officer/Director General of the Board. The Tax Education Division plans and monitors tax education programmes, prepares and updates tax education modules, trains trainers and other relevant activities.

Malaysia's tax education

The overall objective of Malaysia's taxpayer education programme is to promote voluntary compliance amongst citizens and to permanently instil positive social and cultural awareness that paying tax contributes to nation building (Box 16.1).

Box 16.1. **Objectives of taxpayer education in Malaysia**

- Create awareness amongst the public about tax laws.
- Educate taxpayers in their rights and responsibilities.
- Assist and motivate taxpayers in voluntarily complying with tax laws.
- Assist taxpayers in reporting and calculating the amount of tax payable.

Source: Inland Revenue Board of Malaysia.

Tax education programmes are targeted at individual taxpayers, companies, tax agents, employers and potential taxpayers. The IRBM also enhances and improves its service delivery to taxpayers using various approaches and activities to reach out to the public:

- The introduction of online and electronic services to help taxpayers fulfil their tax obligations (Box 16.2). The IRBM also uses social media like Facebook, Twitter and YouTube in carrying out educational activities.
- Talks, seminars, workshops and briefing for all levels of the public, including employees, employers, companies, and university and secondary school students. The aim is to minimise errors in income tax calculations and to encourage the use of the IRBM's e-services (Box 16.2). For example, in 2011, the IRBM held taxation seminars at 22 selected locations nationwide.
- A Business Support Unit which helps owners of small and medium-sized businesses and a Traders' Support Service which offers workshops to small and medium traders on business record keeping, the preparation of simple business accounts as well as tax calculation and payment methods.

- Volunteer tax relation officers in government departments other than the IRBM disseminate tax information to employees. In 2011, a total of 1 616 tax relations officers were appointed and trained by the IRBM.
- Post-budget seminars for IRBM officers to provide first-hand information on changes in tax laws and policy.
- Counters at various fairs and seminars to help taxpayers with any problems they may face in completing their income tax return forms, and to encourage them to use e-filing for speed and convenience.
- Permanent counters in urban transformation centres, where various government agencies are housed in one location to ease and facilitate the general public in their dealings with the government.
- Taxpayers' Service Month (TSM), held in April and June every year. During these months the IRBM intensifies its public promotion and publicity activities via radio, television, print media, website, brochures, etc. The IRBM counters are open longer during the TSM.
- Collaboration with tax practitioners to provide taxpayer education on specialised topics such as transfer pricing.

Announcements and publicity through the media enhance the IRBM's image, increase public awareness and disseminate information on taxation to the public. Advertisements are used continuously, in particular as the deadline for the submission of tax returns draws near. Radio and television airtimes as well as advertising space in local papers are secured to create tax awareness. In addition, the IRBM sponsors a special television series, the sitcom, *Small Mission Enterprise*, aimed at small and medium-sized entrepreneurs that covers tax matters (http://malaysiasme.com.my/products/small-mission-enterprise-sitcom).

Apart from preparing modules and materials for education activities, the Tax Education Division is also responsible for conducting training of trainers for branch co-ordinators. The branch co-ordinators are also given refresher courses to keep them abreast of changing procedures and legal provisions.

Box 16.2. Malaysia's Self-Assessment and e-Filing Systems

The IRBM introduced the Self-Assessment System (SAS) in 2001 for companies and in 2004 for individuals. The aim is to facilitate and not frustrate paying taxes. In 2004, the system was improved through the introduction of the online submission facility for a single category of taxpayers. Today the system provides an e-filing service for 11 different categories of taxpayers.

The online services available under the ez-Hasil web portal include: e-Filing, e-payment, TAeF (Tax Agent e-Filing), e-Daftar (e-Register), e-PCB (for monthly tax deduction from salary), e-DATAPCB (for employers to make payment of monthly tax deducted from employees' salaries), KALKULATORPCB (for monthly tax deduction calculation), STAMPS (for stamp duty), e-Kemaskini (e-Update), e-Lejar (e-Ledgar), e-DATAPRAISI (for prefilled salary information by employers) and e-SPC (for tax clearance letter).

The IRBM has further enhanced its online facility by introducing mobile filing in 2012. This facility enables taxpayers who are always on the go to submit their return forms using their telecommunication devices.

Source: Inland Revenue Board of Malaysia.

Focus on: Tax fun through camps and role play for children

One of the IRBM's key objectives is to increase tax awareness among young people to enable them to become tax-literate citizens. It does so through a series of activities whose emphasis is on fun:

- Tax camps. The IRBM's training arm (Box 16.3), in collaboration with the Ministry of Education, organises educational three-day camp camps for school students. The camp, "Kem Cerdik Cukai", is aimed at students from secondary schools from all over the country. The camp aims to instil a sense of responsibility for paying taxes among the younger generation. It also exposes students to career opportunities in the field of taxation and team-building activities. The camp was first organised in 2011 and has now become an annual affair.

Box 16.3. The Malaysian Tax Academy

The Malaysian Tax Academy (MTA) was established in 1994 as the IRBM's training arm. The MTA's core goal is to train all categories of the IRBM's staff in taxation, audit, specialised technical areas, management and interpersonal skills. The MTA also conducts taxpayer education programmes through talks, seminars and educational camps organised for the public. Among the tax education programmes undertaken by the MTA are:

- National tax conferences. An annual conference aimed for tax professionals, academics, accountants and auditors from both the public and private sector. This annual conference manages to draw in a crowd of almost 2 000 participants each year and is considered one of the major tax education events for the year.
- Tax education camp for students. This nationwide camp is aimed for students from secondary schools from all over the country.
- Study visits. The MTA receives requests from universities, colleges, schools and various other organisations to provide talks on taxation. These talks are usually held at the MTA and the target group varies depending on requests.

Source: Inland Revenue Board of Malaysia.

- Hasil Speech Competition. Organised by the IRBM and the Ministry of Education Malaysia, this annual competition is open to all students in government and government assisted schools.
- Visits to the IRBM headquarters and branches. These visits, conducted all year round, welcome students from institutions of higher learning and external agencies. Visits involve an introductory talk on the IRBM and tax awareness, a briefing on careers in the IRBM and a visit to the IRBM service counters.

- Hasil quizzes are held to assess the impact of information communicated during the tax awareness briefing.
- Junior Tax Officer. Kidzania® is an educational and entertainment centre which gives children the chance to role play different occupations and jobs in more than 60 industries and services. The IRBM is the first government agency to become an official industry partner at Kidzania® Kuala Lumpur. Known as the Tax Office, Kidzania® Branch, this space was officially opened to visitors on 14 September 2013. This allows students aged 6-14 to experience being a tax officer. Junior tax officers watch videos on the role and function of the IRBM and how the government uses tax money. They are guided by supervisors to do a tax calculation through the e-tax system and are overseen while they collect a tax payment from a selected business. At the end of the session the supervisor pays them a salary in the form of Kidzos, a portion of which is removed for income tax purposes!

Impacts

- Wider reach. The tax education talks and seminars reach about 150 000 taxpayers a year.
- Increase in filing. There was an increase of 8.6% in e-filing between 2012 and 2013 (as of 31 October 2013).
- Greater efficiency. The taxpayer education and customer services, especially the electronic services such as mobile filing and e-filing, have increased efficiency and productivity.
- Better customer relations. Through interactions with the customers and the public, the IRBM's emphasis is on promoting and facilitating and giving taxpayers greater choice in how they file their returns. Taxpayers are able to give their feedback and views, enabling the IRBM to improve the services it offers to them.
- Outreach to the next generation. From 2011 to 2013 more than 600 students participated in the children's tax camps, raising their awareness of the responsibility to pay taxes and how taxes help the country to develop.

Box 16.4. Inland Revenue Board of Malaysia (IRBM)

The IRBM's roles include:

- to act for the government in administering, assessing, collecting and enforcing payment of income tax, petroleum income tax, real property gains tax, estate duty, stamp duties and such other taxes as may be agreed between the government and the Board
- to advise the government on tax matters and to liaise with the appropriate ministries and statutory bodies on such matters
- to participate in or outside Malaysia on tax matters.

It has 11 061 staff across its 19 departments, 36 branches, 17 investigation branches, 24 revenue service centres and 2 training centres.

For more information:

Website: www.hasil.gov.my

Taxpayer education address: Corporate Services Department, Inland Revenue Board of Malaysia, Menara Hasil Cyberjaya, Persiaran Rimba Permai, Cyber 8, 63000 Cyberjaya, Selangor, Malaysia.

Source: Inland Revenue Board of Malaysia.

Chapter 17

Mauritius: Building a culture of compliance

Tax Education and Communication Department

This chapter presents Mauritius' taxpayer education programme. It first gives an overview of the activities and their objectives, followed by a focus on one specific element, the initiative on tax awareness at school. It finally looks at the impacts and lessons learnt of the initiative.

The Mauritius tax system is based on universal self-assessment, the aim of which is to create a culture of voluntary compliance. One way of achieving this is by raising awareness through outreach initiatives and education. The Taxpayer Education and Communication Department (TECD) has played a pivotal role in this respect, sensitising taxpayers through a number of well-designed strategies and policies. The TECD is an integral department of the Mauritius Revenue Authority (MRA, see Box 17.2), and is responsible for taxpayer education, helping taxpayers with tax information and assistance, and liaising with the media in implementing its communication strategy. Like other units of the MRA, the TECD has performance indicators and targets to meet.

Mauritius' taxpayer education

The MRA's planning strategy centres on a theme of "fostering a culture of compliance" (Box 17.1). This is one of its essential objectives – to change, through a well-designed educational programme, taxpayers' attitudes and mindsets from "obligation to pay" to "willingness to pay".

Box 17.1. **Objectives of taxpayer education in Mauritius**

- Keep the public informed on all taxation matters (e.g. budget, operations and systems, changes in laws, procedures and processes, new benefits and deductions).
- Provide every means possible for citizens to fulfil their tax obligations in the most convenient and cost-effective way.
- Advise businesses on budget support and various tax allowances approved by the government.
- Show taxpayers how to manage their financial and tax affairs without having to consult a professional (e.g. an accountant).
- Combat corruption and other fraudulent activities such as tax evasion, smuggling and drug trafficking.

Source: Tax Education and Communication Department.

The role of the TECD is to raise taxpayers' compliance level in a sustainable manner and to ensure that every taxpayer becomes an informed person, optimally educated in his/her obligations and rights, with easy access to tax information. Furthermore, it seeks to raise to international standards the level of services offered to citizens and business communities.

The TECD uses a number of key activities to achieve this. Plans are in place for "tax advisory councils" to create a forum for discussing tax matters among MRA officials, industrial and trading operators, taxpayer associations and professionals. The aim of these discussions is to make life easier for taxpayers, while reducing compliance costs and the costs of doing business.

The TECD also has an online presence in the form of the Taxpayer information Online Service (TPOS), which gives taxpayers full access to their personal tax accounts with the MRA, using an individual personal identification number (PIN). Not only are members able to see the status of their account, but they are also able to view up-to-the-minute tax information and messages. Tax messages are also advertised and information disseminated using electronic billboards. Currently, these are located at the entrance of the TECD building, but there are plans to install three more at other strategic locations. The TECD is also installing signposts at government-funded sites such as public hospitals, bridges and public road works, containing messages such as "Your taxes at work" and "Thank you for contributing to nation-building".

Other multimedia tools are also used to disseminate educational programmes geared towards specific target groups. These tools take the form of seminars, workshops, meetings, PowerPoint presentations, videos, posters, brochures, leaflets, guides, publications in the press, radio and TV programmes.

In addition to these key activities, the TECD's strategic plan for 2012-15 includes the following taxpayer education initiatives:

- "Claim your receipt or invoice", a value-added tax (VAT) sensitisation programme using posters, press, radio, television and the MRA website to communicate relevant information.
- A tax information programme for small and medium-sized enterprises, women, the self-employed and informal businesses.
- National Taxpayers' Day, an opportunity to celebrate the taxpayer and offer the public a chance to become better acquainted with the TECD's services. This also involves a number of activities such as a national essay competition for schools.
- A tax education programme for primary and secondary schools (see "Focus On" section below), helped by the use of electronic tools such as e-mail, an interactive website, social networks (the MRA is already on Twitter) and the Taxpayer Information Online Service.
- An MBA course in taxation at tertiary level, with sponsorship for research on tax issues. A collaborative partnership between the University of Mauritius and some foreign universities is sponsoring research and professional writing of tax articles for reputed tax journals and the international press. The MRA also intends to sponsor one research student from the University of Mauritius to do a PhD in a tax-related field of study.
- Informing vulnerable groups of entrepreneurs in rural, informal sectors of tax matters (tax incentives in particular), the VAT refunds on equipment purchased and other benefits provided by the state. Target sectors include fishermen, farmers, beekeepers, horticulturists and pig breeders.

The TECD has a strong media presence, carrying out regular press conferences and meetings to disseminate communiqués and public notices. These are attended by the written press, national radio, television as well as local private radio channels. Radio and television programmes by TECD resource officers in local languages highlight the various tax measures announced in the latest government budget.

Focus on: Tax awareness at school

Today's youth are tomorrow's taxpayers. It is therefore important that they are made aware of the importance and purpose of taxation so as to cultivate a "willingness to pay" attitude rather than feeling "obliged to pay". It is also necessary to ensure a sustained increase in the number of taxpayers over time. Therefore, since January 2012, the TECD has conducted a tax awareness programme for secondary school students.

This programme outlines people's tax responsibilities as law-abiding citizens. It covers all the taxes that citizens must pay, such as the VAT (on all daily consumption purchases), restaurant tax, taxes on liquor and tobacco, fuel tax, income tax and corporate and/or property taxes. The programme also gives an insight into how tax revenue is spent and looks at the unlawful and punishable aspect of tax evasion. However, there is a strong emphasis on cultivating a sense of national duty and patriotism rather than negative feelings towards tax. The aim is to foster a culture of compliance, where citizens see paying taxes as an integral aspect of their relationship with their government. Furthermore, it is hoped that students will act as "MRA ambassadors" by sharing these attitudes with their parents and perhaps even deter them from evading taxes.

At the beginning of each year the TECD, together with the educational authorities, schedules meetings in the secondary schools around the island. The school sessions are conducted by TECD resource officers and consist of three main parts:

- a short PowerPoint presentation
- video and short films about various governmental projects financed from tax revenue
- lively discussions with students and teachers followed by handing out leaflets, posters and stickers.

The TECD brings the following to the respective schools:

- laptop, projector and screen for PowerPoint presentations
- an individual "youth pack" for each student to take home, including an interactive CD with a video clip promoting voluntary compliance, and a corporate video on the MRA
- a short video showing the various projects financed from tax revenues (such as roads, bridges, hospitals, prisons and social centres)
- a CD containing presentations, leaflets and posters plus electronic copies of the MRA annual report, the MRA annual magazine and the MRA newsletter (hard copies of these documents are also provided for classrooms and libraries)
- a link to the MRA's Twitter account
- a link to the MRA's website
- camera equipment for taking photographs and filming the session for newsletters, the local press and for special national TV programmes.

Essay-writing competitions are also organised for secondary and university level students.

Whilst these initiatives are conceptualised and implemented solely by the MRA with no outside partnering, they rely on the co-operation of the educational authorities. The initiative involves four employees at the national level; none of these officers are given any specific training. The total cost is approximately MUR 100 000 (USD 3 200).

Impacts

The initiative has been evaluated via feedback forms as well as through conversations with students and teachers. These show that it has been very effective in raising awareness and building a positive attitude toward tax among young people:

- A future generation is being reached. Since the launching of the initiative in 2012, 17 schools have been covered – thus approximately 1 500 students have been exposed to this tax programme.
- Awareness is growing. With this number of students being reached, there is a growing understanding and preparedness for the future among the next generation of taxpayers.
- Perceptions are more positive. Attitudes towards tax have become more positive and there is a perception among students that the government is spending their tax money wisely. Students also feel a greater sense of fairness over their national tax contribution. It would seem that they hold a healthier view of tax than their parents.
- A culture of tax compliance is emerging. Given that the largest demographic in this initiative is students, who will only become taxpayers in approximately five years' time (or longer), it is not possible to say just how effective this initiative has been in raising actual tax compliance. Nevertheless, the moral obligation to pay taxes voluntarily has been strengthened, which would strongly suggest there should be an improvement within the next five years.

Lessons learnt

Being proactive in promoting tax education is vital to shift people's often very negative attitudes and perceptions about taxes. It is also essential for breaking the cycle that perpetuates these attitudes from one generation to the next.

While there has been no external partnering, the TECD recognises the importance of co-operation with the educational authorities and has made this relationship a successful one. Initially, however, this was not the case and there was a considerable amount of resistance from most quarters – for example, school authorities were reluctant to give the MRA a slot because they felt there were already too many subjects on the syllabus and that students were over-burdened.

Next steps

The fact that Mauritius' educational authorities have renewed the MRA's slot in the extracurricular programme indicates their satisfaction with this initiative. The MRA intends, therefore, to continue with this initiative and to widen its influence as much as possible so as to cover all secondary schools in the country. It also intends to undertake a survey to assess how the programme has been received by the school authorities, the students and the parents. A "lighter" version of the programme is being developed to cater to primary school students aged 10 and 11. This will make use of more visuals such as videos, cartoons and colourful posters so as to keep these students engaged.

Box 17.2. Mauritius Revenue Authority (MRA)

The MRA is the government's main revenue collecting agency. It is a fairly new organisation, having started operation in July 2006. The MRA groups under one roof various former governmental departments: income tax, the VAT and customs, as well as taxpayer education and communication. The MRA's vision is to be "a world-class revenue authority respected for its professionalism, efficiency, fairness, integrity and its contribution to the nation's economic and social development."

In addition to implementing tax laws and regulations, the MRA is also actively seeking to combat tax evasion, smuggling and drug trafficking in a step towards upholding and protecting the country's trading integrity.

For more information:

Website: www.mra.mu

Twitter account: http://twitter.com/MRA_services

Source: Tax Education and Communication Department.

Chapter 18

Mexico: Teaching tax in higher education

Tax Administration Service

This chapter presents Mexico's taxpayer education programme. It first gives an overview of the whole programme and its objectives, followed by a focus on one specific element, the teaching on tax in higher education (National Tax Education Programme). It finally looks at the impacts and lessons learnt of the initiative.

Educating taxpayers has long been a priority for Mexico's Tax Administration Service (*Servicio de Administración Tributaria*, SAT; see Box 18.3). The SAT's central administration launched the National Tax Education Programme in 1997; around 130 officials are now employed in this programme. The SAT sees citizen participation as a vital element of tax education and seeks to engage the public through a variety of activities.

Mexico's taxpayer education

Tax education in Mexico is based on an educational process that aims to change individual conduct in order to have a positive impact on Mexican society (Box 18.1). Through education, a new culture is generated aimed at building citizenship, expressed partly as the voluntary fulfilment of tax obligations.

Box 18.1. Objectives of taxpayer education in Mexico

- Increase voluntary, prompt, committed and responsible compliance with tax obligations.
- Improve the image of public institutions and ensure social awareness and acceptance of the tax system.
- Challenge the current context of low citizen engagement in public affairs and tax contribution.
- Raise people's awareness of citizenship from an early age and throughout the entire education process.
- Inform citizens about how tax revenue is generated and used, in order to change perceptions.
- Encourage active public participation in government activity.

Source: Tax Administration Service.

Many different measures have been launched since the National Tax Education Programme came into force in 1997. The main activities include:

- designing courses on tax in university teaching programmes (focused on later)
- adding tax content to free textbooks distributed by the National Education System
- using a friendly "Fiscalito" mascot to bring tax issues to the public's attention
- promoting and disseminating services among taxpayers
- educating primary school students in years 5 and 6 (ages 9-11)
- holding conferences at universities and tours of regional offices
- running various cultural exhibitions and fairs for children and their parents, offering activities to inform and encourage good habits
- running the SAT areas at the recreational centre "Kidzania®" in Cuicuilco (Box 18.2).

The programme has several public partners, such as the Secretariat of Public Education, the Secretariat of Economy, the Mexican Institute of Social Security, the

Instituto del Fondo Nacional de la Vivienda para los Trabajadores (Institute of the National Housing Fund for Workers), the *Instituto Mexicano de Contadores Públicos* (Mexican Institute of Public Accountants), the *Colegio de Contadores Públicos* (Public Accounting School), as well as public universities. Private partners include the *Desarrollo Empresarial Mexicano* (Mexican Business Development) and private universities.

Box 18.2. **Tax at Kidzania®**

This 14 000 m² activity centre for children is in the form of a scaled-down town, where children can drive electric cars and take part in hundreds of activities. It includes two SAT areas – a tax office and a customs office – where children learn about the value and source of the "fruit of your labour", or wages, and how taxes are related to social welfare. Every year around 1 million people visit Kidzania®, 70% of them children under 16.

Source: Tax Administration Service.

Focus on: Teaching tax in higher education

Engaging with and educating future finance and accounting professionals will provide them with the tools they need to interact with the tax administration during their career. This is the basis for the SAT's educational strategy, launched in 2004: a win-win strategy to produce informed and receptive tax professionals who could play a key role in improving tax awareness and compliance.

To carry out this initiative the SAT linked up with the Federal Institute for Education, resulting in a "collaboration agreement" between the Secretariat of Finance and Public Credit and the Secretariat of Public Education. The agreement is to co-ordinate civic education matters through tax education programmes for the public, including promoting programmes that will strengthen a culture of civic participation within the national education system.

This collaboration led to a curriculum that is relevant for university courses at all levels. It was developed as an approach to build professional competence and aims to train professionals to be ethically responsible and socially committed in their careers.

The SAT also collaborated with the Mexican Institute of Public Accountants to draw up a *Tax Training and Information Guide* for the curriculum. The content is divided into units, each with a specific learning objective, and provides learning activities, teaching suggestions and a glossary of frequently used fiscal terms.

The course was piloted at the well-known National Autonomous University of Mexico (UNAM or *Universidad Nacional Autónoma de México*), considered to be the best in the country (QS, 2012). Once the UNAM technical committee had reviewed the *Tax Training and Information Guide* to check that the contents conformed to the syllabus, the subject was added to the syllabus for the final semester of each degree course.

As soon it was included in the UNAM curricular programme, the SAT's 68 regional offices began to roll out the tax curriculum strategy across the nation, arranging support and collaboration agreements between the SAT and educational institutions in various regions. The public and private educational institutes which now offer the course include the *Instituto Tecnológico de Estudios Superiores* in Monterrey; the *Instituto Mexicano de Contadores Públicos A.C.* (Mexican Institute of Public Accountants) in Acapulco; the

Universidad Popular Autónoma del Estado de Puebla and the *Benemérita Universidad Autónoma de Puebla*, in Puebla; and the *Universidad del Valle de México*, at federal district level. A partnership with the European Union's international programme EUROsociAL has supported these projects in Mexico.

The subject was initially designed to be taught on-site, but can now also be accessed through distance learning; and while it was originally conceived for accounting and administration undergraduates, it is now available for all university students without requiring any prior tax knowledge.

The National Tax Education Programme involves two sets of public officials working together: 68 SAT officials and 68 public education officials. The SAT officials are responsible for supervising the project's design and operation across the country, and for reaching agreements with universities to include the tax training and information curricula in their study programmes. The role of the public education officials is to teach the tax curriculum at the various universities and institutions. All staff are subject to a permanent review process, as well as training courses to keep teachers up to date with regulatory tax amendments.

There are costs related to all design and instrumentation tasks related to the Tax Education Programme performed by SAT public officials. Private institutions pay for the printing and dissemination of educational material. The printed work has a recovery cost of approximately USD 12. However, in order to ensure that all material is accessible to alumni, the electronic version of this material is available on each university website.

Impacts

The National Tax Education Programme has been assessed by programme co-ordinators from the SAT and public education using basic statistics on the number of actions executed, offices visited, attendance by educational level, events held, and so on. Focus groups provide qualitative assessments, and students who received the training and who then registered in the taxpayer census are followed up a year later as case studies. These assessments show:

- Good involvement by educational institutions. To date, the tax course has been taught to 18 graduating classes in 71 universities.
- A growing public interest in tax matters. The degree of citizen participation indicates an interest in tax matters.

To give a wider perspective, a comparative international study was conducted through the Inter American Center of Tax Administrations (CIAT, *Centro Interamericano de Administraciones Tributarias*). The CIAT carried out a questionnaire-based survey of tax administrations in Latin America as part of a best practice study on implementing tax education. The results have yet to be published.

Lessons learnt

The main challenge in rolling out this educational programme across Mexico is the fact that tax education is not a state policy. This has been a hindrance to implementation as it is difficult to obtain institutional support to commit resources. Links between institutions in the public sector also need to be strengthened, as well as links with private institutions.

Further developments are planned for tax education in universities:

- the possibility of graduating with a degree in tax education
- tax education specialisation or certification programmes
- a certificate in tax education programme for SAT officials
- tax counselling courses
- competitions and artistic activities run by regional SAT offices
- including fiscal education in degree courses for teachers
- creating a new course on tax in micro, small and medium-sized companies for future entrepreneurs
- offering students registration in the taxpayer census in anticipation of joining the job market.

As well as these plans for higher education, the National Tax Education Programme has scheduled several other initiatives, including:

- Volunteers: creating citizen groups to help encourage civic awareness and a tax-paying culture. Groups could help improve social cohesion and public spaces.
- Citizen observatory: an area where the public can have a say in the use and allocation of public resources, and for holding public officials accountable for their decisions.
- Citizen caravan: permanent or travelling shows with a tax education theme, to attract all age groups through puppet shows, plays, concerts, recitals, exhibitions, and so on. Topics could cover building citizenship and the common good. This could also help to promote Mexican artists.
- Open day: tours will be offered to the general public to find out how a customs authority works. This will help to make national customs authorities transparent, inform people about customs, and stress the importance of declaring what type of merchandise is entering and leaving the country.

Box 18.3. Mexico's Tax Administration Service (SAT)

Mexico's SAT is a public federal body with headquarters in Mexico City. It has 36 000 public workers and 68 regional offices, each acting as a taxpayer helpdesk for the largest cities in each state or region. As a fiscal authority it is detached from the Secretariat of Finance and Public Credit, enjoying managerial and budgetary autonomy and technical independence to issue its resolutions.

Its mission is to administer tax collection at the federal level, control merchandise coming into and leaving the country, manage risks and encourage adequate and voluntary compliance with all tax obligations.

For more information:

Website: www.sat.gob.mx

Taxpayer education e-mail address: civismo.fiscal@sat.gob.mx

Source: Tax Administration Service.

Reference

QS (Quacquarelli Symonds) (2012), *QS University Rankings: Latin America*, QS, London, available at: www.topuniversities.com/latin-american-rankings.

Chapter 19

Morocco: Educating children about taxes

General Directorate of Taxes

This chapter presents Morocco's taxpayer education programme. It first gives an overview of the whole programme and its objectives, followed by a focus on one specific element, the education of children in tax compliance. It subsequently looks at the impacts and lessons learnt of the initiative, followed by an outlook on next steps.

The Kingdom of Morocco strongly encourages all citizens to honour their tax obligations so that each taxpayer, according to his or her means, helps to fund services to the community. The Ministry of the Economy and Finance has put in place various measures to enable citizens to meet their obligations, including specific targeting of the informal sector. Civic education is one of the strategic objectives of the ministry's General Directorate of Taxes (DGI; see Box 19.4), which uses taxpayer education extensively to reach taxpayers, potential taxpayers and future generations (Box 19.1).

In Morocco, taxpayer education falls under the general responsibilities of the ministry's DGI. There is no specialised unit for taxpayer education.

Morocco's taxpayer education

Key activities include:

- participation by the DGI in public information salons or forums, e.g. e-gov, and the Moroccans Residing Abroad salon (see Box 19.2)
- publishing press communiqués on filing tax declarations and paying taxes, as well as on changes in tax legislation, deadlines, statistics, tax procedures and tax measures introduced under the Finance Law
- producing and updating guides, website and brochures (for example, the *Guide for Moroccans Residing Abroad*)
- participating in national TV and radio broadcasts and producing radio and television adverts in connection with awareness-raising and popularisation campaigns
- maintaining a website and e-mail messages, mainly to economic operators (accounting experts, Moroccan General Confederation of Business [CGEM], chambers of commerce)
- sending out information letters on specific changes to the tax system
- holding information tours for the DGI's partners by managers from central and regional units
- meetings with business
- working closely with the Ministry of National Education, as well as with individual schools
- organising community and cultural events.

Morocco's efforts to engage the informal economy are particularly noteworthy. Budget 2011 introduced targeted legal and administrative provisions to encourage informal businesses to register. Following this a large advertising campaign was launched by the DGI to promote tax compliance. This involved press releases, TV spots and radio messages, awareness-raising and information days. It was especially targeted at professional associations and accountants to raise awareness and encourage them to help informal businesses enter the formal economy.

Box 19.1. Objectives of taxpayer education in Morocco

- Promote taxpayer compliance.
- Provide information on taxpayer rights and obligations.
- Improve the image of the General Directorate of Taxes (DGI).
- Explain why taxes should be paid.
- Increase the number of citizens who pay taxes.
- Empower citizens to engage in discussions on the use of tax revenue.
- Increase citizens' tax literacy.

Source: General Directorate of Taxes.

The DGI has signed agreements with the Moroccan General Confederation of Business and with the Federation of Chambers of Commerce, Industry and Service to establish a partnership based on trust and with the particular aim of promoting civic responsibility towards tax. Other partners are economic operators (accounting experts, the CGEM, etc.), regional investment centres, etc.

Box 19.2. Taxpayer education for Moroccans residing abroad

Every year the General Directorate of Taxes puts in place an information and guidance system for Moroccans residing abroad (MRAs). While many of these people visit family in Morocco regularly, they tend to stay for only a short period especially during the summer months and usually in remote locations. A specific strategy is therefore needed to reach them:

- The DGI has published a special brochure specifically for the MRAs, which is distributed in its reception offices and published on its website.
- A reception and information unit for the MRAs is set up in July and August every year in the Hassan II Foundation for Non-Resident Moroccans, which provides support for non-residents while in Morocco and promotes co-operation on economic, social and cultural affairs for the MRAs.
- A welcome desk dedicated to receiving and taking care of the MRAs is also set up every summer in every regional tax administration.
- The DGI participates in the annual national MRA day in August and in the National MRA Salon – also in the summer – organised by the Ministry for Non-Resident Moroccans.
- The DGI also participates in the MRA gatherings organised in a number of European countries (Belgium, France, the Netherlands, Spain, etc.) by the Ministry for Non-Resident Moroccans and a number of other bodies (Hassan II Foundation, *Agence de l'Oriental*, etc.).

Tax officials respond to queries sent in from citizens residing abroad, putting them in touch with the relevant regional director.

Source: General Directorate of Taxes.

Focus on: Educating children in tax compliance

As noted above, civic education is one of the strategic objectives of the DGI's new vision. In April 2013, a Framework Agreement was signed between the Ministry of the Economy and Finance and the Ministry of National Education aimed at educating younger generations in the role of taxes. This partnership is an important step towards the extension and expansion of a pilot programme that had previously only been conducted in the region of Rabat. The co-operation aims at raising the awareness of children and young people about taxpayer compliance and to acquire the elementary notions of citizenship. Beyond this, the programme encourages them to ask relevant questions to their parents in order to raise their taxpayer awareness as well.

The 2013 agreement is the culmination of several small-scale actions focusing on children. These began in 2000 when the DGI gave a presentation on the obligations of tomorrow's citizens at the second children and young citizens' salon. From 2001 to 2005, 20 schools in Morocco's capital Rabat participated in seminars to familiarise children with the concepts of solidarity and living in society. In 2005, a partnership with the University of Rabat trained DGI managers in teaching in exchange for these managers providing courses on taxation to university students. In addition, a brochure in French entitled "What the Word 'Tax' Means" was distributed to the Academy of Rabat by the Ministry of National Education. Every year between 2005 and 2011, the DGI participated in the children and young citizens' salon, as well as in forums organised by Moroccan engineering schools (Akhawayne University, *École Mohammedia des Ingénieurs*, ENSIAS, etc.). In 2011, television advertising spots and radio advertisements were recorded and screened in order to increase tax compliance and civic responsibility. The main actor chosen for the spot was a young boy of school age. Five series were broadcast at ten-day intervals three times a day during peak viewing hours. And 200 posters and 200 brochures were distributed.

Box 19.3. Explaining taxes to children – theatre script (excerpt)

Sami: Look Yasmine! It's the Directorate General for Taxes our teacher told us about in the civic education class yesterday. We go past it every day and had no idea what it was!

Yasmine: Yes you're right Sami, before that lesson I knew nothing about taxes.

Sami: I wonder if you can remember what the teacher told us.

Yasmine: Of course I can! He said that we all live together in our country and that, depending upon how much money we had, we all had to contribute to the shared cost of developing our country.

Sami: So a tax is a sum of money that each citizen, depending upon his or her income, pays to the state which then spends it on things that benefit all of us.

Yasmine: And what does the state spend its money on?

Sami: On all public services and infrastructure such as schools, hospitals, sports stadiums, theatres, roads, airports, etc. And don't forget that the teacher also told us that there were several different types of tax.

Note: Translated from French.

Source: General Directorate of Taxes.

In 2010, steps were taken to formalise these actions by signing a preliminary agreement with the Ministry of National Education. To transform this idea into a realistic project, a forum was organised by the Ministry of the Economy and Finance. This brought together all the actors on the tax stage: members of parliament, representatives of the government and the administration, economic operators and social actors, representatives of various national and international bodies, experts and academics from both Morocco and abroad. Together they carried out a comprehensive reflection of the Moroccan tax system informing how best to teach it in schools.

The initiative involves the DGI's Communication Department in conjunction with the Training Department and the Reception and Co-ordination Offices. The Communication Department implements activities and prepares communication products for the media and target audience. The Training Department is responsible for designing training programmes and making them available to teachers. In total 20 employees are involved (12 at the national level and 8 at the regional level).

The total annual costs of the programme are approximately MAD 700 000 (approximately USD 83 000), funded entirely from the allocated operating budget. However, the DGI does not have its own communication budget as the budget of the Communication Department is managed by the Ministry's Resources Directorate, together with the expenditure and investments of other departments or directorates.

Impacts

Overall, the initiative has received satisfactory feedback from its partners and the printed press. However, no survey or external assessment has been conducted.

- Increase in taxpayers. The number of newly registered taxpayers has risen to over 12 400 and continues to rise; tax compliance is improving.
- Greater tax literacy. The initiative has resulted in a slight increase in taxpayer literacy (i.e. the skills to pay taxes).
- Perception changes. The public is becoming aware that the tax administration is reaching out to taxpayers to strengthen a relationship of transparency and trust. Furthermore, the initiative has contributed to a slight increase in the perception that taxpayers are treated fairly and transparently by the tax administration.

Lessons learnt

The education initiative has allowed the DGI to measure the degree of taxpayers' ignorance about tax matters, prompting it to step up communication with taxpayers in terms of teaching and informing. Above all, the taxpayer education programme has boosted the confidence of taxpayers and has enhanced the image of a tax administration that works in partnership with taxpayers.

However, in general while taxpayer education undoubtedly calls for action to raise awareness, what is most needed is to improve the quality of the services provided and to foster a relationship based on trust with taxpayers through clear legislative texts and transparent procedures.

A main challenge for the initiative was the high cost of audiovisual broadcasts. However, broadcasts can be made free of charge if the DGI can demonstrate that they are in the national interest; if not they must be paid for (though with lower fees).

Next steps

The initiative would have a greater impact if extended to the whole country; currently only the Rabat region is targeted. A first step in that direction has been undertaken with the April 2013 signing of a partnership agreement between the Ministry of the Economy and Finance and the Ministry of National Education with concrete actions to be taken by each party currently being discussed.

Beyond, this, the DGI is planning to work in close collaboration with the private and public sectors as well as with civil society in order to help the citizens of tomorrow.

Other planned activities are the production of short audiovisual broadcasts explaining taxes in simple terms, as well as organising tax information days once a year to present the various missions performed by the DGI and the taxes it manages.

Box 19.4. General Directorate of Taxes (DGI)

The mission of the DGI (*Direction générale des impôts*) is to establish the taxes levied by government (corporate tax, income tax, value-added tax and stamp duties); collect those taxes; ensure that the law is properly applied; and to manage, on behalf of local authorities, the bases for the three local taxes (professional tax, tax on furnished accommodation and local authority services tax). Its role is both to deter and to instruct while safeguarding taxpayers' rights.

The DGI has a staff of 4 870 officials, divided between central and external, and regional departments. It follows a devolved territorial organisation made up of 15 regional tax directorates.

For further information, see: www.tax.gov.ma.

Source: General Directorate of Taxes.

Chapter 20

Mozambique: Together building momentum for good citizenship

Revenue Authority of Mozambique

This chapter presents Mozambique's taxpayer education programme. It first gives an overview of the whole programme and its objectives, followed by a focus on one specific element, the "Together We Make Mozambique" campaign. It subsequently looks at the impacts and lessons learnt of the initiative, followed by an outlook on next steps.

The government of Mozambique has been carrying out root and branch reforms to its customs and tax since 1996 as part of the Government Finance Reform Strategy to boost revenue collection. The goal of the reform programme is to simplify and modernise the tax system, aligning it with the best regional and international practices in order to broaden the tax base, substantially increase revenues, and thus contribute to reducing the budget deficit.

The process of assigning unique tax identification numbers (NUITs) began in 1999. Yet by 2006 only 388 924 taxpayers had been registered. This was the year that Mozambique's Revenue Authority was created (AT or *Autoridade Tributária de Moçambique*; see Box 20.3), and it has spearheaded tax policy implementation and led to an improvement in tax and customs revenue.

Mozambique's taxpayer education

The AT sees tax education as a high priority, aiming to make all citizens familiar with tax matters (Box 20.1). A national taxpayer education strategy was set out in the Mozambique Revenue Authority's Strategic Plan for 2009-10, and continues to be implemented. It focuses on compliance with taxpayer obligations, taxpayer rights and reviving a taxpaying culture.

Box 20.1. **Objectives of taxpayer education in Mozambique**

- Increase reach by training a cadre of tax education and tax popularisation disseminators.
- Publicise tax topics through the mass media.
- Raise awareness of the importance of tax compliance for the sustainable development of the country.

Source: Revenue Authority of Mozambique.

Target groups:

- all citizens
- businesses in both the formal and informal sectors
- public and private educational institutions
- various civil society organisations
- the media
- youth organisations
- religious institutions
- municipalities
- banking institutions
- AT partners with local authority agencies to carry out its tax education programme, as well as using Mozambique's television, radio and newspapers.

Focus on: The "Together We Make Mozambique" campaign

One of the actions set out in the AT's 2009-10 Strategic Plan to broaden the tax base was to run a national Tax and Customs Education and Popularisation of Taxes campaign. The campaign has evolved and was incorporated into the Strategic Plan for 2011-14, along with other strategies to substantially increase tax revenues.

The week-long, annual campaign was formally launched on 12 April 2010 under the slogan "Together We Make Mozambique". The objective was to ensure that all citizens become familiar with tax matters, and it focused on taxpayer compliance, taxpayer rights and reviving a taxpaying culture. It particularly targeted the informal sector, encouraging businesses to register for an NUIT and benefit from the Simplified Tax for Small Taxpayers (ISPC), introduced in 2009 (Box 20.2).

Box 20.2. Simplifying tax to attract the informal sector

In line with best practices for making it easier for people to pay their taxes, the Revenue Authority introduced the Simplified Tax for Small Taxpayers (ISPC) in 2009. This tax formed part of the government's 2005-2009 Five-Year Plan, which sets out strategies to simplify and improve the tax system, and to adopt measures to broaden the tax base. The strategy includes revising tax regimes to make them more transparent and attractive to potential taxpayers – particularly those running micro- and small businesses – to ensure their contribution to tax revenues and government spending. The ISPC has been used to mobilise registration, particularly in the informal sector, which still represents a significant percentage of the Mozambican economy. From 2007 to the end of 2012, nearly 119 000 further potential taxpayers were registered with the ISPC.

Source: Revenue Authority of Mozambique.

The campaign aims to:

- involve all sectors of society
- use all means to demonstrate the importance of tax
- use culture and sports as vehicles.

It involves creating and publishing reports on taxes and their importance; debates and interviews on television and radio; articles in the printed press; the production and distribution of information pamphlets, brochures and bulletins, merchandise (t-shirts and caps) and CDs with tax messages; road shows and tax education caravans.

Partnerships are a key way for the AT to improve media coverage. It has developed memoranda of understanding with various sectors, particularly businesses in both the formal and informal sectors; public and private educational institutions; various civil society organisations; media agencies; youth organisations; religious institutions; municipalities; and banking institutions. These memoranda commit parties to work together to raise awareness of the importance of tax and compliance with tax obligations for the country's sustainable development. Employees of individual partners, such as the Ministry of Health or Radio Mozambique, are then selected and trained as tax education and popularisation disseminators to share information on tax issues amongst their peers.

The campaign is co-ordinated by the Chairman of the Revenue Authority through the Department of Communications and Image (GCI). The GCI works directly with the AT's registry sector and the provincial delegations, which in turn oversee the administrative areas, district departments and community leaders (Table 20.1).

The AT taxpayer education strategy also involves local AT agencies across the entire country in training the disseminators. To date, over 36 000 disseminators have been trained.

Table 20.1. **Number of Revenue Authority employees involved in the tax education campaign in Mozambique***

Sectors involved	Number of employees involved
Department of Communications and Image Department	40
Registry	100 (2 at each tax office and 1 in each tax area)
Provincial delegations	22
Total	162

Source: Revenue Authority of Mozambique.

Note: * Working on the campaign is not a full-time commitment; employees have other tasks and responsibilities.

The role of AT staff is to carry out tax registration, assign taxpayers their NUITs, and provide support and assistance to taxpayers in local communities. Their more public role is to train disseminators on tax and custom issues, present talks to foster taxpaying among the general public, and participate in television and radio programmes.

AT employees in three regions (Northern, Central and Southern) have been trained as tax disseminators. At least 2 employees are expected to be trained in each of the 11 provincial delegations in 2013. Therefore approximately 22 trainers will be instructed in all the tax modernisation projects, such as *Janela Única Electrónica* (JUE; Electronic Single Window), e-tributação (e-taxation), tax payment machines – and other tools provided by the World Customs Organization (WCO) and African Tax Administration Forum (ATAF). They will be given a certain amount of autonomy in training disseminators, as well as in running tax education campaigns.

The tax education campaign costs (Table 20.2) include mass communication – television, radio and print agencies (production and insertion of advertising spots, reports, press releases, and so on); posters; publications (information bulletins, magazines and supplements); tax education manuals; tax and customs information pamphlets and brochures; and tax popularisation initiatives using culture, recreation and sport. Some of the costs were for training tax and customs disseminators, in partnership with youth associations, non-governmental organisations (NGOs), district administrations, administrative areas, settlements, markets and other legitimate spokespeople.

Table 20.2. **Approximate costs of the tax education campaign in Mozambique, 2010-12**

Year	MZN* costs	USD costs	Exchange rate
2010	50 927 550	1 818 841	28.00 MZN/USD
2011	82 494 469	2 946 231	28.00 MZN/USD
2012	19 725 383	657 512	30.00 MZN/USD

Source: Revenue Authority of Mozambique.

Note: * Mozambique meticais.

Impacts

The "Together We Make Mozambique" campaign and related taxpayer education activities seem to have been successful, particularly in increasing taxpayer registrations. Between 1999 and 2006, roughly 390 000 people registered as taxpayers. By 2012, this number had increased fivefold (Table 20.3). This represents an average registration of 285 988 NUITs every year since the creation of the AT and the launch of the tax education and popularisation campaign.

Table 20.3. **Annual registration of taxpayers in Mozambique, 1999-2012**

Description	1999-2004	2005	2006	2007	2008	2009	2010	2011	2012	Total
Individuals	126 373	116 047	96 409	186 324	187 185	183 219	257 434	321 292	498 440	1 972 723
Businesses	10 597	2 522	36 976	3 554	4 384	4 933	5 068	6 286	7 814	82 134
Total	136 970	118 569	133 385	189 878	191 569	188 152	262 502	327 578	506 254	2 054 857
Cumulative total	x	255 539	388 924	578 802	770 371	958 523	1 221 025	1 548 603	2 054 857	x

Source: Revenue Authority of Mozambique.

Note: x: not applicable.

Lessons learnt

AT staff met with a number of challenges in carrying out the tax education campaign. It was difficult to engage all spheres of society, since Mozambique is a vast, linguistically diverse country which also has low levels of literacy. Some areas were too remote and inaccessible to reach. Many people are resistant to changing their attitudes to taxation due to a culture of non-payment and widespread ignorance of the importance of tax revenue for the country's development. People find it difficult to visualise the impact it would have for them and the country if more people paid tax.

Next steps

Several improvements are planned for the current tax education campaign, including:

- reaching all spheres of society through the use of local languages
- training people with sight deficiencies (and translating manuals into Braille), and training people with hearing deficiencies and those who are mute, to enable them to contribute to the campaign
- producing manuals in comic strip format
- inserting tax material into all mass media, including community radio; installing a radio and television studio to broadcast AT advertising materials, reports and notices
- inserting tax and customs material into primary and secondary school textbooks and introducing courses on these subjects.

Box 20.3. The Revenue Authority of Mozambique

The Revenue Authority (AT) was created in 2006. Its mission is to collect revenues and to implement its tax policies with effectiveness, efficiency and equity, including customs duties. It aims to make it more convenience for taxpayers to meet their obligations, as well as to protect the economy and society. It is responsible for executing fiscal and customs policy, managing the Revenue Authority's departments, planning information systems, training staff, and researching and designing tax and custom policies. The AT has 4 270 personnel in 374 offices around the country, in both urban and rural areas.

For more information:

Website: www.at.gov.mz

Taxpayer education e-mail address: gcimagem@at.gov.mz, gcimagem@gmail.com

Source: Revenue Authority of Mozambique.

Chapter 21

Nigeria: Tax soap opera

Nigerian Federal Inland Revenue Service

This chapter presents Nigeria's taxpayer education programme. It first gives an overview of the whole programme and its objectives, followed by a focus on one specific element, the television soap opera "Binding Duty". It finally looks at the impacts and lessons learnt of the initiative.

Taxpayers are usually confronted with messages on tax that are overly technical and not explained in an accessible way. If messages are presented in a more engaging fashion, taxpayers can understand the issues at stake, and will be more motivated to pay their taxes. With this in mind, the Nigerian Federal Inland Revenue Service (FIRS) has developed several strategic initiatives that aim to make tax messages more appealing to taxpayers.

Nigeria's taxpayer education

The FIRS has a dedicated taxpayer education unit with a major emphasis on one-on-one or face-to-face engagements (Box 21.1). The Communications Department is responsible for taxpayer education across the mass media and undertakes a range of initiatives in this area.

Box 21.1. **Objectives of Nigeria's taxpayer education**

- Explain the different kinds of taxes that citizens are required to pay, and how, when and where to pay them.
- Show the benefits of paying taxes.
- Increase the rate of voluntary compliance.
- Empower citizens to engage in discussions on the use of tax revenue.

Source: Nigerian Federal Inland Revenue Service.

The FIRS works with the Nigerian media and various public and private institutions to deliver a range of key activities, including:

- radio programmes in the five main Nigerian Languages (Igbo, Hausa, Yoruba, Pidgin and English) broadcast by the main radio stations
- a tax-themed television programme shown on all the major television stations (see below)
- tax movies in the genre of "soap operas," emphasising the different areas and types of taxes, and the need for taxpayers to pay their taxes
- weekly pages in 13 of the major Nigerian newspapers with articles, news and information about tax
- advertising campaigns on different areas and aspects of taxation, such as value-added tax (VAT) and withholding tax, using a multiplicity of different media as well as stakeholder engagement sessions, road shows, etc.
- seminars and workshops for taxpayers
- the use of social media (such as Facebook and Twitter)
- working with higher education institutions, secondary schools and elementary schools
- contests and awards.

Target groups include:

- micro, small, medium and large enterprises
- residents within the Federal Capital Territory and in the military and police (personal income tax).

Focus on: The television soap opera "Binding Duty"

"Binding Duty" is a 30-minute television soap opera, of which 26 episodes have been produced to date. The programme aims to reach out to taxpayers in a relaxed, enjoyable and non-confrontational manner, reminding them of their responsibility to pay taxes, and also increasing tax literacy and compliance.

The programme has a compelling script that conveys accurate messages on taxation in an engaging way that resonates with viewers. Episodes demonstrate with dramatic flair how the old order of inefficient and corrupt tax collection has changed, that it pays to be compliant, and that everyone has a responsibility to contribute to the development of their community and country. Talented actors, including well-known faces from the Nigerian film industry ("Nollywood"), were cast to enliven and creatively interpret the script. Finally, a variety of regional, national and state television stations were selected to broadcast the series across all the regions of the country.

Box 21.2. **"Binding Duty" – Example: *What Goes Around* (Season 1, Episode 4)**

Subject: Tax education

Sub text: The old order has changed/As you sow you shall reap

Synopsis

Because of his special relationship with the girl in the Accounts Department, a young man on Youth Service, Gboyega Cole, discovers that the company he hopes to work for after Youth Service has been cheating on taxes, especially the Education Trust Fund. But the fact does not become crucial until he is denied employment by the company. Ironically, the company has refused to employ him because the boss considers him a half-baked graduate. Gboyega's relationship with his heart throb is not the only thing that is threatened but a career also. He reports the company to the Federal Inland Revenue Service. It is probed and found guilty.

Source: Nigerian Federal Inland Revenue Service.

A professional production company, Quest Communications, was selected to interpret and translate tax messages into a form appropriate for a television drama. Quest became a key partner for the FIRS. Quest provided the technical expertise required to implement the job as well as various other logistics, while the FIRS ensured that the tax content was accurate and that the messages were communicated clearly to viewers and taxpayers.

Eight FIRS staff worked on the project. A cross-section of staff from different tax departments was also involved, especially during the workshop preceding the development of the script. During the production phase, tax enforcement experts were involved to provide advice and to cross-check materials.

The initiative has cost approximately NGN 80 million (approximately USD 500 000), funded entirely by the allocated operating budget.

Impacts

- Wider reach. With a weekly audience of 50 million, the programme has been very successful in raising awareness of taxation among ordinary citizens. “Binding Duty” has been watched by a total of 80 million citizens across Nigeria.
- Greater taxpayer literacy and sense of moral obligation. People’s skills for paying taxes have improved, as has their sense of moral obligation to pay taxes “voluntarily”. People feel that other taxpayers are paying their fair share and that taxpayers are treated fairly and transparently by the tax administration.

Lessons learnt

The complete outsourcing of the entire production process was considered to be both an advantage as well as a challenge. The lack of control over production led to many unanticipated issues cropping up, as well as delays in scheduling. Close supervision and involvement in the production process by the FIRS team helped mitigate these issues.

The FIRS plans to continue the programme. Experience from the first series should allow greater efficiency in future production, which will develop different angles and production lines.

Box 21.3. Nigeria’s Federal Inland Revenue Service (FIRS)

The FIRS’ main responsibility is to access, collect and account for taxes on behalf of the federal government.

With approximately 150 offices across Nigeria’s 6 regions, the FIRS’ mission is to operate a transparent and efficient tax system that optimises tax revenue collection and voluntary compliance. Its vision is to deliver quality service to taxpayers in partnership with other stakeholders and make taxation the pivot of national development.

For further information, see: www.firs.gov.ng

Source: Nigerian Federal Inland Revenue Service.

Chapter 22

Peru: Master Strategy for Tax Education

National Tax and Customs Administration

This chapter presents Peru's taxpayer education programme. It first gives an overview of the whole programme and its objectives, followed by a focus on one specific element, the Master Strategy for Tax Education. It subsequently looks at the impacts and lessons learnt of the initiative, followed by an outlook on next steps.

As with most developing countries in Latin America, domestic revenues are insufficient to cover Peru's public service needs, particularly those of the poorest citizens. This is mainly due to the many people who fail to pay their taxes, either deliberately – to avoid having to pay money they prefer to keep for themselves, or unintentionally because they are confused or uninformed about the need to pay tax. This conduct is directly related to the absence of a citizen culture-based education, that emphasises abidance with the law, the value of the common good and a conviction that everyone needs to contribute.

In 2005, Peru's National Tax and Customs Administration (*Superintendencia Nacional de Administración Tributaria* or SUNAT; see Box 22.3) identified taxpayer education as a key institutional priority for bringing about change. A Customs and Tax Culture Management Unit was created in December 2012 to continue and strengthen taxpayer education activities.

Peru's taxpayer education

Taxpayer education in Peru is aimed at all citizens, but with a specific emphasis on young people and their teachers. The goal is to develop a sustainable tax education strategy (Box 22.1). This currently involves two main projects: teaching tax culture in schools and tax culture in higher education. Interested SUNAT staff can be trained through a virtual course entitled "Citizen Awareness at School". This course gives staff the tools to facilitate and implement tax education programmes in schools.

Box 22.1. Objectives of taxpayer education in Peru

- Promote tax and customs compliance through user-friendliness, stronger tax awareness and risk avoidance.
- Promote economic development and social inclusion.
- Educate people on the social purpose of taxation, i.e. the social benefits derived from paying taxes.
- Raise taxpayers' awareness of the negative impacts of tax and customs offences for the whole community.

Source: National Tax and Customs Administration.

The subject of taxation is taught in all faculties of education and also forms part of schools' and universities' extracurricular recreational and artistic activities (Box 22.2). There has been a concerted effort to improve teachers' skills and commitment for teaching the subject, and tax education teaching material has been developed. Tax essay competitions profile tax matters.

SUNAT also runs a School Payment Receipt Raffle, through which educational institutions can win a prize of USD 300 000 on average to assist them with their various needs. This highlights to teachers, students and their parents the importance of payment receipts and discourages informal economic activity. A similar initiative – School Certifications – encourages fifth-year secondary school students all over the country to demand payment receipts when making a purchase or requesting a service.

At a more general level, modern media such as mobile phones, websites and social media platforms are employed to raise awareness and keep the public informed. In all of these initiatives, SUNAT strives towards the provision of high-quality services.

Box 22.2. **Ayni the penguin tax mascot**

Ayni the Humboldt penguin is an endangered species. "*Ayni*" means "work for the common good" in Quechuan, and the character is a useful emblem for tax work with children. An international tax education seminar arranged by EUROsociAL in Buenos Aires inspired SUNAT to organise the Ayni Educational Circuit in Lima's main zoo. This hugely successful activity teaches children the value of public goods and services, the social role of taxation and the importance of asking for payment receipts. The circuit has since been replicated in schools and fairs all over the country.

For more information, see: http://aulaprimaria.sunat.gob.pe/index.php/quien-es-ayni (in Spanish).

Source: National Tax and Customs Administration.

Focus on: The Master Strategy for Tax Education

SUNAT realised early on that to reach the public it had to begin by teaching all Peruvian children the advantages of taxation and of civic responsibility.

To do this, tax content needed to be brought into the educational curriculum. This has involved a long-term partnership with the Ministry of Education (which covers schools and universities), as well as the general education sector and various other institutions.

This collaboration led to the signing of an Inter-Institutional Co-operation Agreement with the Ministry of Education in July 2006 to include tax awareness content in the curricular programmes of the country's three basic education departments: the Department of Initial Education, the Department of Primary Education and the Department of Secondary Education.

This agreement was just the first step in a long and evolving process of adapting the national curricula. In the meantime, a full-scale organisational effort was also carried out by the Ministry of Education and SUNAT to train teachers in the importance of incorporating tax matters into their syllabus. By the end of 2008, an imminent change in the national curriculum was announced. However, a reshuffle of key Ministry of Education staff meant that new staff had to be convinced once again to include the subject of tax in the curriculum.

The eventual outcome of this long process of deliberation was that in 2009, tax culture subjects became compulsory for all students from preschool up to secondary. That same year, a course was designed to ensure quality teaching of tax matters following the new national curricular design. Since 2010, three half-day workshops have been included to help teachers construct concepts based on their prior knowledge. This ensures that the topics are more directly relevant to each teacher. In 2012, a virtual course was included. A web portal has also been created to make relevant materials accessible to all teachers and students in primary and secondary education (www.cultura.sunat.gob.pe).

In addition to these strategic activities, from 2009 SUNAT also launched a range of informal measures for children and older students to reinforce what was being taught in the classroom. These included the School Payment Receipt Raffle and the School Certifications project, both described above.

A multi-task team of professionals was put together to start up the programme. The number of team members varied between 2005 and 2012 from 5 to 13. The team is headed up by a co-ordinator, whose role it is to manage all national planning and to disseminate and edit all material.

The fact that decision making is decentralised in the education sector meant that SUNAT needed to create a co-ordinator network of SUNAT staff all over the country to implement and co-ordinate the national educational programme, both regionally and locally.

Impacts

Tax education programmes aim to shift behaviour over the long term and as such should not be assessed in the same way as specific short-term projects that aim for a quick boost in compliance, for example. An ideal measurement approach that will hopefully be applied in the future should strictly focus on the areas of intervention, and use baselines against which to measure medium- and long-term progress towards the objectives of the Ministry of Finance and tax administration. An evaluation of children's attitudes should be entrusted to the Ministry of Education as part of its functions.

- A large number of children reached. Around 8 million students have been taught this course in preschool, primary and secondary schools all over the country.
- A great increase in teachers trained. Since 2008, SUNAT has directly trained 14 935 teachers.
- Opportunities to learn through play. More than 200 000 children now enjoy entertainment/educational circuits and plays that teach tax awareness.
- Greater awareness of the need to curtail the informal sector. The Payment Receipt School Raffle has attracted 3 864 schools, which have trained their educational communities (parents, teachers and students) to demand receipts from merchants in order to curtail informal economic activity.

In 2011, the initiative obtained significant recognition when it became a finalist in the Public Management Good Practice Prize. Thus, annual competition is arranged by "*Ciudadanos al Día*" in Peru and backed by the Ombudsman. It aims at disseminating and rewarding successful, good practice in the public sector. The initiative was also a finalist in the Public Impact category, which evaluates all activities aimed at achieving citizen momentum to change the institutional framework for the better.

Lessons learnt

The Ministry of Education usually takes longer to make decisions than SUNAT because new content for children needs to be weighed, reflected upon and proven. The signed agreement was of significant benefit, but perseverance, creativity and constant effort on the part of SUNAT was also required to keep the momentum towards the decision to incorporate tax issues in the national curricula.

Another challenge was that SUNAT-qualified teachers were inconsistent in how they applied tax subjects in the classroom. This was ascertained during the presentation of student projects.

Tax education, given its medium- and long-term results, is not always considered an institutional priority despite its formal presence in all goals and indicators. This is why continual effort is required to encourage awareness amongst internal and external authorities. In particular, the subject needs to be institutionalised within the Ministry of Finance and tax administrations in order to avoid taking a step backwards, reducing staff and not ensuring content continuity.

Next steps

In 2013, a new institutional strategic objective – Leadership of Tax and Customs Awareness amongst Citizens – led to the creation of a Customs and Tax Culture Management Unit.

Box 22.3. Peru's National Tax and Customs Administration (SUNAT)

Peru's SUNAT is a specialised technical body under the Ministry of Economy and Finance. It has functional autonomy as well as its own technical, economic, financial and administrative budget. Its mission is to promote tax and customs compliance through user-friendliness, stronger tax awareness and risk generation. This involves the management of integrated processes, intensive technology use and a committed, unified and competent team that is able to provide excellent services. There are 12 000 employees and offices are located at all urban headquarters, throughout the country's 26 regions.

For further information:

Tax education website: http://cultura.sunat.gob.pe

Facebook: www.facebook.com/CulturaAduaneraTributaria

E-mail address: educa@sunat.gob.pe

Source: National Tax and Customs Administration.

Chapter 23

Rwanda: Celebrating the taxpayer

Rwanda Revenue Authority

This chapter presents Rwanda's taxpayer education programme. It first gives an overview of the whole programme and its objectives, followed by a focus on specific elements – the Taxpayers' Day, tax friends clubs and tax advisory councils. It finally looks at the impacts and lessons learnt of those initiatives.

In 1997, the government of Rwanda carried out a programme of reforms to restore and strengthen the main economic institutions of the country in the aftermath of the devastating 1994 genocide. Amongst other areas, the reforms set out to revive the tax administration; restore processes for budget preparation, execution and accountability; and build capacity for budget and economic management. The Rwanda Revenue Authority (RRA; see Box 23.2) was established as part of this process, to rebuild the nation's capacity for collecting revenue.

Rwanda's taxpayer education

The main responsibility for taxpayer education falls to the RRA's Taxpayer Services Department, which seeks to foster mutually beneficial relationships with external stakeholders through a variety of taxpayer services (Box 23.1). These include customer education and public relations, primarily organised through the department's Taxpayer Education and Media Divisions. The RRA's administration also extends all the way down to district level to make it easy and convenient to pay taxes locally.

Box 23.1. Objectives of taxpayer education in Rwanda

- Foster voluntary taxpayer compliance through effective taxpayer education programmes and high-quality customer service.
- Optimise service delivery through cross-departmental, team-based working processes.
- Raise taxpayers' awareness of RRA facilities and incentives through strategic public relations activities and a culture of customer care.

Source: Rwanda Revenue Authority.

The first challenge for the RRA, after its establishment in 1997, was to build people's confidence in their government to collect taxes fairly and effectively – and to invest this revenue in the population's best interests. Under the slogan "Taxes for Growth and Development", from 1998 the RRA undertook a series of initiatives to inform and engage Rwandans on the importance of taxes for national development. They highlighted the government's development-related investments to show how taxes provide the resources for public services and infrastructure that benefits the public.

This campaign has changed focus three times since 1998:

Stage 1 (1998-2001): Early efforts focused on capacity building within the RRA itself, establishing the RRA brand and building trust and confidence among taxpayers and the wider population. At this stage, the RRA used conventional approaches such as brochures and leaflets, as well as novel initiatives such as talk shows (on television and radio), town hall meetings and the introduction of the popular Taxpayer's Day (featured below). Activities and events were scheduled both nationally and regionally.

Stage 2 (2002-06): One of the major landmarks in the RRA's evolution was the launch of its modernisation programme in 2003. The RRA was originally structured around departments based on tax types, but in 2003 it changed to a more functional approach that clustered taxpayer services and introduced a "one-stop shop" system. To improve public tax literacy, the RRA designed more interactive initiatives with a greater focus on dialogue with citizens and taxpayers. For example, tax friends clubs (featured later) were started in educational institutions in high schools in order to instil a culture of tax awareness early on in people's lives.

Stage 3 (2006-present): This stage has involved a drive to improve people's access to tax services, strengthening relationships with different categories of taxpayers and reinforcing the idea of growing a tax culture among young people. To this end, the Ministry of Education created a tax curriculum in partnership with the RRA and the National University of Rwanda (NUR). The partnership is guided by a memorandum of understanding with the NUR on co-operation and capacity building.

Today tax education activities include:

- disseminating legal and technical tax information in a way that is easily understood, for instance through tax clinics tailored to meet the specific needs of customers; participation in public events such as shows and exhibitions; as well as an annual Taxpayers' Day (see below)
- designing and conducting comprehensive taxpayer education programmes on the importance of tax, the role of taxpayers, tax incentives and taxpayer registration
- improving the image of the RRA through increased corporate social responsibility
- finalising the establishment of tax advisory councils (TAC; see below) at the district level
- generating written information and guidelines for taxpayers and the general public in simple, clear language, including on tax reforms
- producing promotional radio and television programmes, using drama as a tool to raise the general public's awareness of tax issues
- channelling taxpayers' and partners' complaints through the use of suggestion boxes
- following up tax friend clubs activities in secondary schools, and creating more of these in institutions of higher education
- improving staff skills in the Taxpayer Services Department
- speeding up management complaints and information feedback through a call centre and website
- monitoring customer handling within the RRA Operational Department and other departments.

The Private Sector Federation is a key partner in taxpayer education. A Tax Issue Forum has also been created to enable the business community and the tax administration to discuss issues that need particular attention from both sides.

Focus on: Taxpayers' Day, tax friends clubs and tax advisory councils

Taxpayers' Day is a one-day celebration held every year across Rwanda. Recognising that consistent, high-level political engagement is a critical element of tax education, the President of the Republic of Rwanda officiates at this event. This serves to strengthen links between taxation and national development, promote tax compliance and build trust in the RRA. As guest of honour, the Rwandan President gives awards to the country's best taxpayers – such as those who pay on time and those who provide correct payments – from among those in the highest income brackets, as well as taxpayers on small and medium incomes. During the week leading up to Taxpayer's Day there are various activities geared towards corporate social responsibility, including consultations with taxpayers and stakeholders. A report is published for the event outlining tax revenue amounts and the achievements and challenges faced by the RRA. This initiative has been very successful, and the idea is now being adopted by other countries in the East African Community and beyond.

Tax friends clubs were originally designed for high schools, but are now targeting higher educational institutions such as universities. For this programme, RRA officials visit schools for two-hour sessions to speak and answer questions on how the country spends tax revenue, how students benefit and on Rwanda's various taxation laws. The RRA officials encourage the students to tell their friends, family and businesses about the issues discussed. The RRA also offers internships at the Revenue Authority as prizes to students, gives out research grants and holds essay competitions. These initiatives all help to develop a taxpaying culture in the younger generation, as well as instilling greater tax and personal financial knowledge in young people.

Tax advisory councils were introduced in 2000 and have since been expanded to cover Rwanda's 30 districts. The councils meet on a quarterly basis and involve sector-based opinion leaders at *Umudugudu* level (neighbourhood or village level of administration), chaired by the local mayor. These tax advisory councils have been successful at encouraging citizens to play their part in fighting corruption and smuggling; at educating taxpayers on the need to pay taxes on time and the role that taxes play in development; and in widening the tax base. By working with local administrations, the councils help support the process of fiscal decentralisation and broaden the range of citizens who take part to ensure that business interests do not dominate.

Impacts

- Increase in tax revenue. Tax revenue has improved considerably over the past decade, from below 10% of gross domestic product (GDP) in 2000 to a projected 14% for 2013 (ADB, 2011). Whether or not a causal link can be drawn between tax education and tax revenue, it seems that both tax compliance and the RRA's legitimacy among the population are increasing.
- More positive perceptions. The RRA recognises that its capacity to perform is determined in part by external factors, notably taxpayers' perceptions (Land, 2004). However, it has some degree of influence over these perceptions. The government of Rwanda's commitment to development spending is helping to overcome citizens' reluctance to pay tax. Good examples of popular programmes are the "one cow per poor household" and "one laptop per child". The positive attitudes instilled by these programmes in turn helps to generate revenue for more such investments.

Lessons learnt

The RRA sees tax education as a work in progress, and is consistently trying out new approaches and expanding on those that prove to be effective. Other activities besides those listed above include developing cartoon books (based on a South African Revenue Authority project) and a Tax Issues Forum, in which the RRA and private sector executives meet to discuss tax issues of common interest. There are challenges, however, notably in engaging key stakeholders, including business and civil society; outreach to rural areas; and engaging small and medium enterprises, given the size of the informal sector in Rwanda (Land, 2004).

Box 23.2. Rwanda Revenue Authority (RRA)

The RRA was established as a quasi-autonomous body in 1997. Its mission is to mobilise revenue for economic development through efficient and equitable services that promote business growth. Its vision is to become a world-class, efficient and modern revenue agency that can fully finance the nation's needs.

Its responsibilities are to:

- assess, collect and account for tax, customs and other specified revenues through effective administration and enforcement of tax laws
- collect non-tax revenues
- advise the government on tax policy relating to revenue collection
- perform other duties in relation to tax administration as directed by the Cabinet
- assist taxpayers in understanding and meeting their tax obligations.

The RRA's new logo – a rose in green, blue and orange – symbolises the authority's three main values: unity and equity; growth and development; and prosperity. This logo reflects the tax administrators' renewal of attitude and approaches towards taxpayers in their service delivery, opportunities and best practices.

For more information, see: www.rra.gov.rw.

Source: Rwanda Revenue Authority.

References

ADB (2011), *Domestic Resource Mobilisation for Poverty Reduction in East Africa: Lessons for Tax Policy and Administration*, African Development Bank, Tunis, available at: www.afdb.org/fileadmin/uploads/afdb/Documents/Project-and-Operations/Domestic%20Resource%20Mobilisation%20Flagship%20Report.pdf.

Land, A. (2004), "Developing capacity for tax administration: The Rwanda Revenue Authority", *ECDPM Discussion Papers*, No. 57D, European Centre for Development Policy Management, Maastricht, available at: http://ecdpm.org/publications/developing-capacity-tax-administration-rwanda-revenue-authority.

Chapter 24

Senegal: National Information Days

General Directorate of Taxes and Government Property

This chapter presents Senegal's taxpayer education programme. It first gives an overview of the whole programme and its objectives, followed by a focus on one specific element, the National Information Days. It subsequently looks at the impacts and lessons learnt of the initiative, followed by an outlook on next steps.

The government of Senegal recognises the significant challenges facing the country in raising revenue and fostering investment for development. It recently undertook a comprehensive reform of the General Tax Code (CGI) to put in place a fairer, simpler and more efficient tax system, mindful that a tax system has the potential to either enable or hinder progress. The new CGI (Law 2012-31) enacted at the end of 2012 aims to improve general well-being, make the tax system more favourable for investment promotion and increase its efficiency for mobilising revenue. It includes general tax reductions and efforts to broaden the tax base by drawing in the informal economy.

Informing taxpayers and potential taxpayers of the new tax code is an enormous challenge which is often helped by a good, strong online presence (Box 24.1). In 2013, the General Directorate of Taxes and Government Property (DGID; see Box 24.3) upgraded its website with a new logo and new information and online tools. It also re-energised its existing taxpayer education initiatives, in particular the flagship National Information Days.

Senegal's taxpayer education

The DGID does not have a dedicated taxpayer education unit; its extensive taxpayer education activities are carried out by the Central Communications and Public Relations Bureau in collaboration with other departments, supported by local level DGID officials as required.

Box 24.1. Objectives of taxpayer education in Senegal

- Improve the quality of the services supplied to users, particularly with regard to receiving requests and raising awareness.
- Increase the number of citizens who pay taxes.
- Empower citizens to engage in discussions on the use of tax revenue.
- Increase the tax literacy of citizens.

Source: General Directorate of Taxes and Government Property.

Taxpayer education is aimed at both the corporate sector (large and medium-sized enterprises) and personal income taxpayers. But in addition to this, the initiative has sought to draw in the informal sector as well as the nation's youth.

One of its main strategies for achieving this is through organising national and regional information days, running seminars and workshops, and participating in events such as the Dakar International Fair. There is also the introduction of a Master's degree course in taxation in collaboration with the *Université Cheikh Anta Diop* in Dakar and meetings held with groups of taxpayers on a sectoral basis. The DGID has also recognised the importance of a strong media presence and makes good use of mass media such as national radio (French and national languages), television and newspapers as well as a press campaign over a three-week period (leading up to the tax filing deadline). Information is also disseminated to the public through the Internet site, which contains a tax simulator which has been used extensively since the recent tax reform. The DGID's local offices also initiate taxpayer education activities; for example, the city of Fatick's tax office worked with a community school to raise awareness and promote tax compliance (Box 24.2).

Box 24.2. Taking tax to school

On 9 December 2012, the city of Fatick's Tax Office (CSF) staged a tax march along the city's streets in collaboration with the Khar Ndoffène Diouf middle school to celebrate its 50th anniversary. Staff from the tax office marched alongside teachers and pupils for nearly six kilometres through the streets of Fatick and relayed messages by powerful loudspeakers to promote awareness among local people of the importance of tax compliance.

Marchers wore t-shirts bearing the slogan, "*Payer un impôt, c'est construire une école; payer un impôt, c'est construire un hôpital; payer un impôt, c'est construire mon pays*" ("paying tax helps build schools; paying tax helps build hospitals; paying tax helps build my country").

In a speech at Fatick's central market, Tax Office Head Daouda Badio stressed the need for all citizens to meet their tax obligations. Mr. Badio also took the opportunity to remind Fatick's residents of their duty to set a good example in order to help a former pupil of the Khar Ndoffène Diouf School, none other than the President of the Republic himself, in his mission to build the country. The school's Principal then dwelt on the same theme before giving the floor to one of the teachers, Mr. Faye, who repeated the message in the local Serer language.

The march concluded towards midday at its starting point at the Khar Ndoffène Diouf School, where the Tax Office Head and members of staff gave an in-depth presentation of the CSF's different missions, particularly in the specific areas of government property, conservation, the land register and taxation.

Source: Impôt & Domaines (2013), *Impôt & Domaines*, trimestrial magazine, No. 11, Jan-March 2013.

Focus on: National Information Days

The DGID launched the National Information Days initiative in 2008 in response to a general lack of knowledge of tax regulations as well an unwillingness to comply with tax administration officials. These annual events usually last three days (between the months of May and June) and are organised by each regional office in order to fulfil the needs and concerns of their users.

In an economy characterised by a large informal sector, the initiative aims to broaden the tax base by facilitating tax compliance, both in terms of reporting and paying taxes. The informal sector contains a large number of people who may not have attended school and are not registered in the tax administration's files. In addition, the initiative targets personal taxpayers, privately owned and state-owned corporate taxpayers of all sizes, the country's youth and property owners.

The three information days involve a number of different activities, such as public conferences and information stands, where tax officials receive, inform and guide taxpayers. They also involve national newspapers, interactive radio shows, TV broadcasts in French and local languages and mobile tax units. Furthermore, meetings with taxpayer representatives and between local tax administrations and local taxpayers are held.

Reflecting the high level of political commitment to the DGID and its work on the part of the government of Senegal, the National Information Days begin with an official opening ceremony held in the capital, Dakar, presided over by the Minister of Economy and Finance. This includes information stands in public areas, radio broadcasts and walkabouts by the DGID Director-General to meet taxpayers, followed by a closing ceremony.

The year 2013 saw the sixth Information Days take place. Given the heightened importance of the days generated by the introduction of the new tax code, a central organising committee was introduced to ensure the broadest possible dissemination and participation.

The initiative involves a number of partners in order to reach different groups of citizens and taxpayers. Among these are the media, business organisations, civil society, schools and universities, in particular the Université Cheikh Anta Diop.

The Information Days in the city of Dakar involved 30 employees (20 at the local level and 10 at the national level). There is no specialised training for these employees. Part of the total costs for National Information Day activities are covered separately, and part by the allocated operating budget of the Central Communications and Public Relations Bureau.

Impacts

While there is no formal external evaluation, the impact of the initiative is assessed by feedback from visitors at information stands and by telephone calls.

- An increase in taxpayer awareness. The initiative seeks to target as many citizens as possible. As it also involves mass media, it is difficult to estimate how many people are reached. However, it is considered successful in bringing the new tax reform to the public. There has been a noticeable improvement in taxpayer knowledge (i.e. taxpaying skills).
- Better morale. There is a healthier perception that taxpayers are treated fairly and transparently by the tax administration.
- Greater demand for information. Taxpayers are now more inclined to come and ask the departments for further information.
- Greater tax compliance. Over the last five years tax compliance has somewhat improved.

Lessons learnt

The main lesson learnt from this initiative is that National Information Days provide a platform for public discussion to take place in a positive manner. They place the focus entirely on the issue of tax and its role in society.

The personal involvement of the Director-General helped to overcome certain difficulties.

Financing such events is always a challenge, although this was helped by external private funding which partially covered the cost of the information days.

Next steps

Overall, the initiative has expanded somewhat in size and scope. In particular, in 2013, a number of innovations were introduced, such as visits to taxpayers and deployment of information stands in very busy public areas. Further enhancements are planned, such as themed days for professional organisations.

Box 24.3. General Directorate of Taxes and Government Property (DGID)

The DGID (*Direction Générale des Impôts et des Domaines*) is Senegal's main tax administration headed up by the Directorate-General. The DGID oversees all areas of taxation, including property administration, land use and property registration.

The emphasis of the organisation is on presenting user-friendly, easy-to-access tax compliance to the public. In the light of this, a considerable effort has been made to maintain a strong and presentable online presence through their website, with downloadable tax forms and an online tax calculator.

For more information, see: www.impotsetdomaines.gouv.sn.

Source: General Directorate of Taxes and Government Property.

Reference

Impôt & Domaines (2013), *Impôt & Domaines*, trimestrial magazine, No. 11, Jan-March 2013.

Chapter 25

Singapore: No-Filing Service

Inland Revenue Authority of Singapore

This chapter presents Singapore's taxpayer education programme. It first gives an overview of the whole programme and its objectives, followed by a focus on one specific element, the No-Filing Service (NFS). It subsequently looks at the impacts and lessons learnt of the initiative, followed by an outlook on next steps.

The Inland Revenue Authority of Singapore (IRAS; see Box 25.2) is structured around two themes: customers and capacities. Customers are catered for by the tax management divisions (TMDs), which are responsible for delivering customer-centred initiatives and building technical capacity. Centralised services deal with process capacity, focusing on the delivery of either bulk or specialised processes across different types of tax. Corporate divisions deal with organisation-wide co-ordination and development.

Singapore's taxpayer education

The Corporate Communications Branch, Taxpayer Services Management Unit and the TMDs all work together to deliver effective and timely taxpayer education. The Corporate Communications Branch is responsible for education strategies aimed at both taxpayers and the general public (Box 25.1). The Taxpayer Services Management Unit drives the design and development of taxpayer education through online channels through the use of electronic and mobile platforms. The TMDs work to engage and educate specific groups of taxpayers.

Box 25.1. Objectives of taxpayer education in Singapore

- Ensure taxpayers pay their fair share of tax.
- Enhance voluntary compliance.

Source: Inland Revenue Authority of Singapore.

The tax filing and assessment processes, taxpayer services and education programmes are divided up according to the needs of specific taxpayer groups. The IRAS classes taxpayers into four main categories based on different tax obligations:

- individual income taxpayers
- corporate income taxpayers
- goods and services tax-registered businesses
- property owners.

The IRAS runs a number of activities to educate the public and engage it with the tax system, including the following seminars:

- Auto-Inclusion Scheme (AIS) for employment income. Under this scheme, AIS employers simply submit details of their employees' salaries to the IRAS electronically. Seminars are held for employers who are currently not in the AIS, or newly registered companies and businesses. These seminars give an overview of the AIS and show different ways of preparing and submitting employees' income information to the IRAS electronically.
- Corporate tax. Seminar participants are briefed on companies' general tax obligations and how to benefit from common tax schemes, including the Productivity and Innovation Credit (PIC) scheme. Participants also learn how to prepare a tax computation and file an income tax return using Form C-S, a short three-page tax return for small companies.

- The Introduction to Goods and Services Tax seminar is targeted at newly GST-registered businesses. Businesses that have voluntarily registered for the GST must attend this seminar within three months of registration.

Activities also include online learning:

- The e-Learning Portal provides taxpayers with convenient online courses which they can access at any time and complete at their own pace. The courses cover topics ranging from how to use common e-services to an introduction to tax. Each course is designed to be interactive and easy to understand through the use of video and audio features.
- The Volunteer e-Filing Service is an annual nationwide programme through which the IRAS engages members of the public and trains them to help taxpayers with their e-filing. Volunteers include students, working professionals, stay-at-home parents and retirees. Through this service, the IRAS has worked with 1 400 volunteers to help 49 000 taxpayers e-file their tax forms since 2003.

The IRAS has various ways to communicate with the public about its services. It engages and educates taxpayers through a wide range of media, such as its website, Twitter, Facebook, newspaper articles and advertisements. The Taxpayer Feedback Panel consists of representatives from trade and business associations and individuals from various industries; it is consulted quarterly on new services or tax proposals. Public consultations are held on specific tax schemes to get feedback on various aspects of tax laws. An external consultant conducts surveys biannually to get taxpayers' views on their interactions with the IRAS and on their future requirements.

Focus on: No-Filing Service

The IRAS introduced the No-Filing Service (NFS) in 2007 to make it more convenient and less costly for taxpayers to comply with tax obligations. Under the NFS, taxpayers do not need to file a tax return if their employers have already transmitted their salaries to the IRAS and they claim the same standard set of personal tax deductions each year. These taxpayers simply receive a letter or SMS informing them that they have been selected for the NFS and do not need not to file a tax return unless they have additional income to declare or changes to their relief claims. Their tax bills are sent directly to them.

The IRAS started to engage with taxpayers on the NFS during the design phase to build awareness and acceptance of this new approach. To find out how receptive taxpayers were and to address any concerns, the IRAS sought feedback through various forums, including the Taxpayer Feedback Panel. Taxpayers also had the opportunity to share their concerns about the new initiative during three Taxpayer Focus Group (TFG) sessions, and their input was included in the final launch of the NFS. The TFG comprised a cross-section of taxpayers from all walks of life.

A national publicity campaign was launched to create awareness and understanding of the NFS, including newspaper articles and mailouts to taxpayers. Taxpayers received a letter explaining the NFS with a list of frequently asked questions (FAQs), and a dedicated helpline and email address were set up for NFS enquiries.

Implementing the NFS only required minor changes to the IT system to exclude the NFS group of taxpayers from receiving their tax returns; the costs of meetings and the publicity campaign were covered by the normal operating budget. Only two extra employees were needed, to staff the dedicated helpline and email inbox. All frontline staff were trained in handling enquiries about the NFS.

Impacts

- Significant take-up of the NFS by taxpayers. The NFS began with a pilot group of 45 000 taxpayers in 2007; this had expanded to 1.13 million taxpayers by the year of assessment 2013.
- Benefits to taxpayers and the IRAS. The large number of NFS taxpayers who do not need to submit returns reduces the load on the e-filing system and allows a better service for those users who do need to log on.
- Greater efficiency. Since there are significantly fewer paper returns and other relevant documents to send out, the NFS has also improved the IRAS' operational efficiency. Eligible taxpayers' returns can also be processed quickly without any manual intervention.
- Better public perception of the IRAS. The 2013 Taxpayer Survey shows that 97.6% of taxpayers surveyed are satisfied or very satisfied with the IRAS' level of service; 13.3% of these taxpayers are willing or very willing to say positive things about the IRAS.
- More compliant taxpayers. The percentage of individual taxpayer returns filed on time rose from 89% in 2008 to 94% in 2012.
- The NFS recognised externally. The NFS was awarded a bronze medal, beating 12 other public agencies, at the prestigious PS21 ExCEL "Simple Ideas, Extraordinary Results" Convention on 1 November 2007. This annual convention recognises public agencies' efforts in contributing significantly to the civil service by improvements and innovations in their work.

Lessons learnt

The IRAS recognised that taxpayers are likely to have a number of common queries when a new initiative is introduced. A list of frequently asked questions (FAQs) was therefore attached to the NFS letters. This helped to reduce customer contacts with the IRAS, as taxpayers were also able to share the list of FAQs with family and friends.

It was clearly important to people to be reassured that they were not breaking the law by not filing a tax return, since the majority of NFS taxpayers who contacted the IRAS were seeking confirmation that they were not required to file. The IRAS therefore stepped up its public communication of this fact as well as adding a sentence of reassurance in the NFS notification letter.

Next steps

In 2011, the IRAS began sending SMS instead of letters to NFS taxpayers who had provided a mobile phone number. The recent proliferation of mobile devices means that taxpayers find text notifications more convenient than letters.

Box 25.2. Singapore's Inland Revenue Authority (IRAS)

The IRAS was established as a statutory board under the Ministry of Finance in 1992 and now has 1 800 staff. Its vision is to become the leading tax administration in the world, a partner for taxpayers in nation-building and economic development, and an excellent team of competent and committed people. Its mission is to:

- act as an agent of the government and provide service in administering, assessing, collecting and enforcing the payment of taxes
- advise the government and represent Singapore internationally on tax matters.

For further information:

Website: www.iras.gov.sg

Taxpayer education address: taxqueries@iras.gov.sg (individual income tax enquiries)

Source: Inland Revenue Authority of Singapore.

Chapter 26

South Africa: Mobile tax units

South Africa Revenue Service

This chapter presents South Africa's taxpayer education programme. It first gives an overview of the whole programme and its objectives, followed by a focus on one specific element, the South African Revenue Services' Mobile Tax Units (MTUs). An additional section provides information on the staffing and costs of the initiative. It subsequently looks at the impacts and lessons learnt of the initiative, followed by an outlook on next steps.

The South African Revenue Service (SARS; see Box 26.2) has long understood the importance of public tax awareness for achieving a culture of tax compliance. SARS has taken a lead role in taxpayer education, introducing a variety of initiatives ranging from targeted seminars to longer term outreach activities. One of these is SARS' mobile tax units (MTUs) described below.

SARS' taxpayer education falls under the remit of Branch Operations, whose Education and Campaigns Unit supports the SARS compliance programme and ensures that selected taxpayer and future taxpayers groups – individuals, employers, small business owners, school children, government as employer and government employees – are the recipients of data-driven education and campaigns to improve tax compliance.

South Africa's taxpayer education

Engaging taxpayers to increase compliance and the revenue base is a priority for SARS, which is working to enhance its outreach, education, service and enforcement (Box 26.1). SARS runs targeted campaigns for specific tax measures, identified through data analysis of taxpayers and potential taxpayers operating informally. One specific target is small and medium contractors and sub-contractors working in the construction sector; the aim is to assist employers with their pay-as-you-earn (PAYE) reconciliations and improve value-added tax (VAT) compliance through the physical verification of business applications. SARS offers seminars and co-operates with businesses to encourage them to register as taxpayers and assists them with tax compliance.

Box 26.1. **Objectives of taxpayer education in South Africa**

- Explain why citizens should pay tax and how tax revenue is used.
- Show taxpayers how to be independently compliant (e.g. e-filing).
- Reach taxpayers in even the most remote rural areas through mobile tax offices.
- Make taxpayers aware of their obligations, make it easy to meet them and assist them where they are in support of the organisation's Compliance Model.

Source: South Africa Revenue Service.

SARS extends its reach by maintaining a presence in shopping malls and other points of service, especially during tax season; through MTUs (see below) to reach taxpayers in rural areas; and by co-located services in other government institutions that work in areas where SARS is less visible.

SARS also reaches millions of taxpayers through TV and radio, explaining the importance of good fiscal citizenship and showing taxpayers how to become tax compliant. In particular, SARS has a relationship with the TV station eNews Channel Africa (eNCA). An annual eNCA Tax Day reaches 3 million viewers. During this, SARS' employees offer tax clinic services, assisting eNCA staff with their tax affairs while SARS executives and the commissioner conduct interviews promoting tax compliance. The same happens during Primedia Tax Day where SARS assists its affiliated radio stations, Talk702 and Cape Talk. The reach is equally wide as the television station. This partnership has given SARS access to many more taxpayers.

Partnerships are key for SARS. It works with regional and local government institutions to assist their constituencies with tax matters and compliance. It reaches future taxpayers through academic institutions and schools, and it also co-operates with civic associations, private entrepreneurs, businesses and business organisations. For example, in the construction sector many sub-contractors operate informally, outside of the tax base. By working with the construction sector associations, SARS runs educational campaigns to improve compliance standards and disseminate legislative information to construction companies.

Focus on: SARS' mobile tax units

SARS developed a Location Strategy (2009) to determine the extent of the need to expand its footprint in areas where there was no organisational presence. This detailed analysis of its presence across the country identified the need for a stronger presence in rural areas, where there are few SARS offices. SARS decided to explore the use of converted vehicles as mobile offices as an innovative and cost-effective way to reach the neediest areas identified in the analysis (the provinces of KwaZulu-Natal, Eastern Cape and Limpopo). These MTUs would help citizens register as taxpayers, receive education on why taxes should be paid, increase the number of citizens who pay taxes and increase citizens' tax literacy while providing them with the technical know-how to be tax compliant.

A trial run in 2009 began with one MTU. This proved a success and made the case for more MTUs to be set up in regions where SARS offices were thin on the ground. By 2011, the process had progressed and three additional MTUs had been sourced and were ready to use. In September 2011, after a three-month testing phase, the three MTUs were launched for the filing season. This made the service available to thousands of taxpayers and resulted in increased compliance. Without these mobile units, taxpayers would have to travel hundreds of kilometres to deal with their tax matters. SARS decided to procure six more MTUs (which were to be launched in 2013).

Running in tandem with the deployment of the MTUs, SARS made efforts to co-locate its staff in existing government service centres (such as health, education, the military and the police) throughout the country to provide services to the public without building an entire parallel infrastructure. This helped alleviate queues at branch offices and reduced the costs to the taxpayer. It also allowed SARS to visit the employees of these government departments in their workplace to help them become tax compliant.

SARS teams have established good relations with local and community media, including print media and newspapers, in order to publicise MTU activities and locations in particular regions.

Staffing and costs of the programme

To date, the Education and Campaigns Unit has employed some 300 people with varying skills and for various time periods. About 30 staff members consistently service taxpayers via the MTUs (2 at national level and 28 regional staff). This number will increase given that SARS has procured six new MTUs, which will need to be staffed from regional offices.

This new initiative has meant that employees need training to integrate the MTUs into existing SARS systems. Employees also need to have a working knowledge of all tax types (income tax, VAT, PAYE and so on) in order to advise and assist taxpayers. To achieve this, monthly online training is provided to keep staff informed. Staff operating the MTUs have to also be comfortable with information technology as the MTUs operate via satellite connections.

To operate the current three MTUs costs SARS ZAR 306 200 per month (approximately USD 30 000). These costs include:

- satellite costs
- fuel costs
- equipment (printers, scanners)
- maintenance.

These costs exclude human resources and staff accommodation when employees travel from one area to the next.

Impacts

The initiative has not yet been externally evaluated. However, the automated SARS data collection system is able to capture changes in taxpayers' perspectives. SARS also commissions research annually to establish taxpayer satisfaction with the organisation's initiatives. Since the launch of the first and subsequent MTUs in September 2011 and December 2012, the scheme has achieved the following results:

- Improved reach. A total of 77 367 taxpayers have visited the MTUs at 601 centres with an average of 128 taxpayers per location. Those visiting the MTUs did so to register as taxpayers, to submit tax returns, to check tax statuses and to reconcile companies' PAYE accounts.
- Increased number of registered taxpayers. Since introducing the MTUs, SARS has seen growth in the tax register – with an average of 2 000 rural-based registrations per annum.
- Greater tax literacy. There has been growth in the number of taxpayers able to complete their tax obligations independently by making use of SARS' e-filing, as taught, in part, by the MTUs.
- Improved tax "morale". There has been an improvement in people's sense of moral obligation to pay taxes "voluntarily". This is evident by a yearly increase in people submitting their tax returns on time, for example a 7.7% increase from 2012 to 2013. There are also more positive perceptions that taxpayers are treated fairly and transparently by the tax administration, and that other taxpayers are paying their fair share. By taking tax to the people, SARS is seen as a caring organisation.

Lessons learnt

It cannot be taken for granted that taxpayers know how to fulfil their tax obligations; as new tax measures are introduced and the tax register grows, additional taxpayer education is necessary. Whilst e-filing allows for greater independence, "taking tax to the people" has helped raise tax compliance since taxpayers seem more comfortable with face-to-face interaction.

The main challenge for the MTUs has been a technical one – the accessibility of the SARS systems through satellite communications. Satellite coverage is not always optimal, especially in some of the rural areas. This often results in long queues of taxpayers waiting to be served. To resolve this, SARS has had to build strong relationships with its IT counterparts so as to ensure a quick response when MTUs are deployed to rural areas.

Next steps

To reach more people in rural areas, SARS procured six more MTUs for deployment during 2013. The six new MTUs have been equipped with wireless connections allowing them to expand their coverage.

Box 26.2. South African Revenue Service (SARS)

SARS is the main tax collecting agency in South Africa, responsible for all national taxes, duties and levies. It is also responsible for facilitating trade and protecting South African borders from illegal importation and exportation of goods. While it is a tool of the state, its administrative functioning is autonomous.

SARS places a high value on customer-oriented service, ensuring the taxpayer has every means by which to exercise tax compliance in a transparent and equitable way. There are approximately 15 000 employees currently, 51 SARS branch offices and 57 customs offices. There are also three mobile tax units currently in operation, with plans afoot for the procurement of another six.

For more information:

Website: www.sars.gov.za

Taxpayer education address: jkhumalo2@sars.gov.za

Source: South Africa Revenue Service.

Chapter 27

Turkey: Simplifying rental income returns

Turkish Revenue Administration

This chapter presents Turkey's taxpayer education programme. It first gives an overview of the whole programme and its objectives, followed by a focus on one specific element, the initiative to simplify rental income returns. An additional section provides information on the staffing and costs of this project. It finally looks at the impacts and lessons learnt of the initiative.

The Turkish Revenue Administration (TRA; see Box 27.2) has a broad range of initiatives that reflect the importance it places on tax education for enhancing voluntary compliance (Box 27.1). These are informed by gathering baseline information through surveys, and collecting suggestions and comments from target audiences. Two especially noteworthy initiatives are the Vergibilir Training Programme for Children and the Tax Communication Centre.

Box 27.1. Objectives of taxpayer education in Turkey

- Collect adequate revenue through the principles of justice, impartiality and efficiency to increase social welfare.
- Simplify the tax system and enhance compliance.
- Provide a high-quality service to the taxpayer.
- Become a model administration globally which enhances and embraces every kind of economic structure and activity.

Source: Turkish Revenue Administration.

The Vergibilir Training Programme for Children is designed to raise tax awareness among the upcoming generation. It reaches approximately 4 million primary school children in the third, fourth and fifth grades and presents tax matters in an age-appropriate way. The project is conducted by the Presidency of Revenue Administration in co-operation with the Ministry of National Education. Training sessions are run by 299 trainers selected by the Ministry of National Education from among social science teachers, class teachers and trade school teachers. These trainers are volunteers and are made up of teachers from all 81 provinces. By June 2011, 330 000 primary school students had participated in the training programme. A website in both Turkish and English containing educational and entertaining games, stories and different tax-themed activities has been prepared for children as part of the project (www.vergibilir.gov.tr). A CD – Vergibilir Songs – has also been prepared for primary school students. It promotes family values, school, good hygiene and good nutrition, and also raises tax awareness.

The Tax Communication Centre (TCC), founded in 2006, is the first point of access for taxpayers seeking information from the Turkish Revenue Administration. Affiliated to the Ministry of Finance, it provides tax consultation, motor vehicle tax services and denunciation management – the opportunity for taxpayers to inform the revenue administration about tax evasion or tax crimes committed by others. This is done through a call centre and via e-mail. The TCC began e-mail based consultations for foreign nationals and corporations in May 2012. Due to privacy regulations, this consulting service does not provide any information on liability or information on any personal or corporation accounts. The TCC has been leading the way for other government agencies to establish their own professional call centres.

Focus on: Simplifying rental income returns

In Turkey, as in most countries, people who receive rental income are obliged to declare it on their annual income tax return. However, analysis conducted by the TRA has indicated that of 1.2 million known people receiving such income, several hundred thousand were not declaring it. The TRA identified a number of problems with the existing system which were contributing to this. Because taxpayers had to go to the tax office to declare the rental income manually, it was largely perceived as a waste of time. There were also many incorrect and missing declarations, with the TRA often being unsure whether taxpayers had submitted their declaration or not. Limited audits and insufficient electronic data were also found to contribute to the overall non-compliance. These weaknesses led to the introduction of a pre-filled e-tax return for declaring rental income in March 2012, for the 2011 tax year.

Turkey's pre-filled e-tax programme is simpler, more efficient and more ecological. A pre-filled e-tax return for each taxpayer is constructed from third-party information received by the TRA's data warehouse. Prior to full implementation of the pre-filled, e-tax programme, a focus group was conducted with 50 taxpayers who receive rental income at the TRA's IT centre. The programme was described to them. Their opinions in all matters related to the programme were received, down to the fonts and colours to be used on the form. The programme was then upgraded, notably to simplify the terminology used in the prefilled e-tax form to the extent possible.

When taxpayers declare their statements for the first time, their registration in the tax office is created automatically. Taxpayers then have online access to their pre-filled e-tax return where they can include missing information and/or correct the pre-filled information. All tax changes associated with the modifications are automatically computed on the e-return which is easily submitted online at the click of a button. Taxpayers can then pay the outstanding amount using their credit cards or via Internet banking.

The key objective of the online return is to simplify the tax procedure, making it easier and cheaper for taxpayers to complete their returns, while at the same time ensuring greater accuracy.

The TRA has made full use of modern technology in a bid to promote tax knowledge and tax compliance. The TRA ran a nationwide multimedia publicity campaign to encourage the use of the prefilled e-tax forms by conveying to the public their ease and simplicity. The specific focus was on the older taxpaying population, who generally earn rental income. The campaign involved sending to 1.2 million tax filers an introductory brochure about the pre-filled e-tax return. The TRA also set up information booths at tax offices and shopping malls and joined popular tax forums to provide information and answer questions about this initiative. Newspapers, television and billboards were also used, including a three-day, full-page advertisement with the message "It's Not Worth the Risk" in all national newspapers. The initiative was also mentioned on television in a popular quiz show and on television series, as well as on billboards in airports and in metro stations. Towards the end of the declaration period, reminder messages were sent to taxpayers via SMS.

Less traditional media platforms were also used: the Minister of Finance made a YouTube appeal, inviting taxpayers to use the pre-filled e-tax return. In addition, one of Turkey's most popular comedians presented a funny introductory video which was posted on Facebook and YouTube. He humorously explained the new e-tax initiative, highlighting its innovations. Another campaign targeted older taxpayers in a five-minute sketch in which a grandmother submits her online tax return with the assistance of her grandson. The sketch emphasised that e-tax saves time and money and is user-friendly; it was also shared on Facebook and YouTube.

The prefilled e-tax form initiative involves 25 employees at the national level and 2 000 locally; 1 800 staff received training across 18 regional areas. An additional 5 IT engineers and 20 experts helped to establish the system and match the data. This initiative has reduced pressure on the operating budget as its results and overall contribution have been higher than expected (see below).

Impacts

- Increase in the number of taxpayers. Following the publicity campaign, around 1.2 million people submitted their 2011 income tax return online using the pre-filled system. In 2010, before the pre-filled system was introduced, only around 890 000 people lodged an e-tax return. The rate of increase in the total number of rental income taxpayers was very high; approximately 33%. The online tax service has proved a popular choice, and once informed, the great majority of taxpayers have taken advantage of this pre-filled service.
- Increased benefits for the TRA. The pre-filled online declaration reduces the need for data matching, auditing and tax-dispute resolution. There are fewer discrepancies and amendments for the TRA to follow up because the data entry process is controlled by the taxpayer, who also has the opportunity to confirm and self-rectify the information provided by the TRA and other third parties. It is also expected to have a direct impact on the behaviour of non-filers by drawing them into the system.
- Improved efficiency. The pre-filling system reduces the administrative burden and costs for taxpayers too. Making changes online is less resource intensive than manual checking and because there is less paper used, it is also more ecological. Moreover, paper returns are approximately three times as costly to process as e-returns. Other useful information is downloaded into a summary for taxpayers to retain should they require it at a later stage to declare or to make a claim.
- Increased compliance. Although the initiative has not been externally evaluated, an internal perspective suggests a notable and significant improvement in tax compliance as a result of the simplified tax declaration.

Lessons learnt

An effective nationwide publicity campaign using a range of traditional and new media, including social media, can provide taxpayers and potential taxpayers with the practical tools and motivation to declare their income successfully. The result is improved compliance in a cost-effective manner, and the taxpayer target audience being better known to the TRA.

This is the first such initiative undertaken by the TRA, and it will be continued for the next several years.

Box 27.2. The Turkish Revenue Administration (TRA)

The General Directorate of Revenues was established by law in 1946. In 2005, it was replaced by the Turkish Revenue Administration (*Gelir İdaresi Başkanlığı*). This saw the start of a new period, with the establishment of the Presidency of Revenue Administration as a subordinate but semi-autonomous authority of the Ministry of Finance. The TRA's mission is to collect adequate revenue while pursuing the principles of justice, impartiality and efficiency for increasing social welfare; to help simplify the tax system and enhance compliance; and to provide a high-quality taxpayer service.

The TRA has 1 032 tax offices country-wide and a total staff of 40 244.

For further information:

Website: www.gib.gov.tr

Children's portal: www.vergibilir.gov.tr

Source: Turkish Revenue Administration.

Chapter 28

Uruguay: Tax-themed computer games

General Directorate of Taxation

This chapter presents Uruguay's taxpayer education programme. It first gives an overview of the whole programme and its objectives, followed by a focus on one specific element, tax-themed computer games. It finally looks at the impacts and lessons learnt of this initiative.

Taxes are one of the most important instruments to allow the state to finance its activities and to fulfil its commitments. Uruguay's General Directorate of Taxation (DGI; see Box 28.3) recognises the importance of projecting a healthy image of its tax administration to the public; it does so through various communication strategies. The DGI also seeks to encourage voluntary tax compliance by citizens and to deter tax fraud (Box 28.1). Therefore, tax education is one of its strategic objectives.

Uruguay's taxpayer education

The DGI's tax education programme was conceived in 2003, and implementation began in 2005 through a pilot project entitled "Education for Participatory and Responsible Citizenship".

Box 28.1. Objectives of taxpayer education in Uruguay

- Promote society's tax awareness.
- Encourage values and attitudes such as solidarity, justice, equity and responsibility in children and young citizens.
- Promote responsibility and citizen participation in community social life.
- Fight fraud and tax offences by promoting a healthy and positive attitude to taxation among the entire population, including children.

Source: General Directorate of Taxation.

The programme is backed by a Framework Co-operation Agreement signed in 2006 by the National Administration for Public Education (ANEP) and the DGI. This governs the joint execution of educational programmes on citizenship, including tax awareness.

This collaborative approach has allowed the DGI to develop, jointly with teachers, a range of teaching material (comics and textbooks) that can be used in schools across the country. The DGI also runs workshops for teachers and other educators and provides agreements for jointly developed syllabi for primary and secondary education.

More recently, the DGI has begun creating electronic tax content for schools. For example, a video game allows children to be superheroes travelling in time to resolve an emergency threatening the entire community (see next section). Along a similar line, the DGI puts on a show called "The Time Machine" in a shopping centre at the *Ciudad de los Chicos* that uses a game format to encourage children to be responsible citizens. The DGI also has a stand at the agricultural/industrial exhibition ExpoPrado. The stand is targeted at children, encouraging them to see the relevance of taxes in a playful and entertaining manner.

The DGI's main tax education partners are ANEP, the Council for Basic and Primary Education; the Council for Secondary Education; the Plan Ceibal initiative; the Ministry of Education and Culture; and the Film and Audiovisual Institute of Uruguay (*Instituto del Cine y del Uruguay*). The DGI also uses television, radio and newspapers for its taxpayer education activities and partners with the agricultural and industrial sector.

The programme is currently funded from the national budget, but was initially jointly financed by the European Union, as part of the DGI Updating Project. It subsequently became part of the Tax Management Support Programme with financing from the Inter-American Development Bank.

Focus on: Tax-themed computer games

Plan Ceibal is a social/educational initiative launched in 2007 by the Presidency of the Republic. This inter-institutional project provides a personal laptop to each school child and teacher in all state primary schools across the country. It involves various public bodies in the teaching and technology fields. In 2012, the plan was extended to students and teachers in secondary education and professional technical education (basic cycle). It is currently being extended to higher education students.

Inspired by the One Laptop per Child Project (Box 28.2), Plan Ceibal provides low-cost laptops (called XOs), free software and wireless connections both inside and outside the classroom. These laptops are child-resistant, water- and dust-proof, lightweight and portable. Their dual screen (black/white and colour) allows them to be used both indoors and outdoors, without viewing being affected by the sunlight. A removable card for storage is provided, as well as USB ports and a video camera.

The DGI saw and seized the opportunity offered by this initiative to develop digital tax education content for the Ceibal platform, in partnership with the Council for Basic and Primary Education, the Council for Secondary Education and the Plan Ceibal. The first product was an interactive book generated by primary school teachers. In 2011, the DGI launched the +Ciudadano application. This invites children to improve their city while learning about tax. Along with the fictional character Iván, children visit and improve their own neighbourhood, gradually completing various levels by focusing on topics such as rights and obligations, society, state and tax culture. They discover information which helps them complete the various tasks. In doing so, they improve the public space, while activating entertaining minigames to reward their effort.

Box 28.2. One Laptop per Child

One Laptop per Child is a project supported by the Miami-based One Laptop per Child Association and the Cambridge-based OLPC Foundation, two US non-profit organisations set up to oversee the creation of affordable educational devices for use in the developing world. The aim is empower children through education, by providing each child with a rugged, low-cost, low-power, connected laptop. The project has designed hardware, content and software to allow children to become engaged in their own education, and learn, share and create together. In October 2007, Uruguay placed an order for 100 000 laptops. The country reportedly became the first in the world where every primary school child received a free laptop on 13 October 2009 as part of Plan Ceibal.

Source: One Laptop Per Child website: http://one.laptop.org/stories and Wikipedia (accessed 9 October 2013).

The DGI uses video games to connect with and reach its younger target audience. In 2012, the DGI developed an educational video game for third-year secondary school students in Plan Ceibal. The game takes place in a city hit by strong storms, with buildings demolished and documentation and virtual data belonging to public authorities lost. In this emergency situation, the government asks for help whilst it reorganises its services and a group of young people take on the task of obtaining and distributing resources. The main character handles various community services needing repairs, new constructions, salary payments, furniture, supplies, etc., and takes charge of managing tax collection in order to cover all service needs and make them operable for the entire population. There are levels of achievement and reward, as well as summary screens to see what the student has done, handling concepts such as resources, taxpayers, tax collection, evasion, budget, costs and investment. The video game promotes citizenship through exploring topics such as social co-existence, the state as an organisation and citizen participation, while highlighting the social and economic importance of taxes in the community. Development of this resource was backed up by the Council for Secondary Education (CES) through a group of inspectors and teachers with broad experience in developing teaching materials.

The DGI also created a new Tax Education Portal, accessible via the XO laptops or home PCs. This educational site is specifically geared towards primary and secondary school students, although educational content is also offered for the general public. The portal is divided into three main areas:

- Games to download: two educational applications are available for downloading.
- Online games: a recreational space for learning through play. In Iván vs. Evatrones, children can avoid "*evatrones*" (tax evaders) while collecting tax. In Invincible, children gather as much tax as possible and avoid the evaders while travelling the country. They may also encounter situations where no tax receipts are provided (DetectIVAte).
- Homework statistics: this attractive and user-friendly space contains technical information for a broader target audience, such as tax system information and statistics for university students or even journalists. In general, the information is grouped into three main areas:
  - The relevance of tax: data charts to explain the role of tax in society, the tax system and taxation in Uruguay. General information is also provided on tax receipts.
  - DGI tax collection: interactive graphs to explore DGI tax collection performance and changes in composition. These graphs illustrate: aggregate tax collected during the current; gross tax collected by the DGI every year with all taxes classified into income, property and consumption; performance of gross tax collected; and gross domestic product (GDP), showing how tax collected by the DGI has been surpassing GDP performance.
  - Evasion: interactive graphs which analyse tax-evasion trends in Uruguay (as a percentage of potentially collected value-added tax (VAT), the total tax collected by the DGI, and as a percentage of GDP), and a dynamic graph showing trends in VAT evasion in Latin American countries over the last ten years.

Impacts

- Tax messages to a wider audience. The launch of +Ciudadano extended the tax education programme to 100 000 fifth- and sixth-year school students and to all teachers in the country's state primary schools. Extending the programme to secondary schools has reached another 40 000 third-year basic cycle students, as well as social and civic education teachers in state secondary schools. This means that the Tax Education Programme is universally known amongst children in primary and secondary state schools throughout the country.

- Greater educational resources. Over six years, Plan Ceibal has delivered laptops to more than 575 000 students and teachers. Its educational platform contains more than 8 500 educational elements and the project has trained 40 000 teachers in the use of technological resources. Since the very beginning, Plan Ceibal has been welcomed by most of the population.

- Greater communication. Plan Ceibal has provided global information, communication and culture to a far greater sector of the population, irrespective of their socio-economic standing or geographic location. Given that children take their laptops home and that Internet access is available in public spaces, the plan opens up these communication paths to the children's family members.

- Reduced inequality. An evaluation of Plan Ceibal shows that providing universal computer access in schoolchildren's homes can overcome traditional inequalities. This change could not have been brought about through the market (Rivoir and Lamschtein, 2012).

Lessons learnt

The DGI initially used a very traditional tax education model (mainly involving books), which demanded a huge and expensive effort by the administration. Its reach was a limited audience: even though books were distributed all over the country, many were simply left in the school libraries. Permanent training was required, as well as costly supervision and assessment.

By making the most of the opportunities offered by Plan Ceibal and new technologies, the DGI has ensured constant and flexible access to tax content by young people. This new model is innovative, it encourages collaboration and social integration amongst children, teachers, educational centres and families, and enables them to participate in new national and international learning communities.

Plan Ceibal is a model example of a good use of taxes. Financed by resources generated by the tax system, it is itself a vehicle to develop programmes that strengthen tax awareness amongst citizens, thereby obtaining more resources for contributing to development.

Next steps

The DGI will focus its future activity on developing new content and electronic educational resources, such as:

- A special application for basic, or primary, education students (ages 6-9) will extend the tax education programme through Plan Ceibal. It will also be available on the DGI Educa Portal.

- A resource for pre-university students – available on the Ceibal platform and DGI Educa Portal – will encourage responsibility and citizen participation in community social life.

- Online activities to provide primary and secondary school teachers with technical knowledge and information on available resources. The idea is to help teachers and educators with teaching tax and citizenship subjects.

Box 28.3. General Directorate of Taxation (DGI)

The DGI (*Dirección General Impositiva*) falls under the Ministry of Economy and Finance. The DGI's General Technical Secretariat is in charge of all activities related to tax education and is responsible for collecting state resources. The DGI encourages voluntary compliance by taxpayers whilst upholding their rights, acting with integrity, efficiency and professionalism in order to provide a good service to society.

The DGI is staffed by 1 400 public officials, 40% of whom are professionals, 29% of whom are technicians, 30% are administrative assistants and 1% in services. It has offices in 19 geographical departments, and its head office is in the capital city of Montevideo. It also has 5 regional offices and 40 representative offices distributed all over the country.

For more information:

Website: www.dgi.gub.uy

Website, Tax Education Programme: www.dgi.gub.uy/educa

E-mail, Tax Education Programme: culturatributaria@dgi.gub.uy

Source: General Directorate of Taxation.

Reference

Rivoir, A. and S. Lamschtein (2012), "Las tecnologías digitales frente a los desafíos de una educación inclusiva en América Latina" [Digital technologies facing the challenges of inclusive education in Latin America], Chapter V in Sunkel, G. and D. Trucco (eds.), *Ceibal Plan, "Un caso de usos de las tecnologías de información y de las comunicaciones en la educación para la inclusión social"* [Case study of information and communications technology in education for social inclusion], Information Society Alliance Programme, ECLAC and the European Union.

Chapter 29

Zambia: Tax chat

Zambia Revenue Authority (ZRA)

This chapter presents Zambia's taxpayer education programme. It first gives an overview of the whole programme and its objectives, followed by a focus on one specific element, the tax chat on the radio. It subsequently looks at the impacts and lessons learnt of the initiative, followed by an outlook on next steps.

Zambia has come a long way in reforming its tax system, particularly improving legislation, lowering tax rates and simplifying procedures. As part of this, the Zambia Revenue Authority (ZRA; see Box 29.4) has understood that improved knowledge of the tax system can change taxpayers' attitudes and tax morale, and lead to greater tax compliance.

Zambia's taxpayer education

Taxpayer education has become an important component of the ZRA's efforts to build a taxpaying culture in Zambia (Fjeldstad and Heggstad, 2012). The Taxpayer Education Unit is a new unit within the ZRA's headquarters (Box 29.1); prior to its introduction, taxpayer education and tax services were combined, and this is still the case for the provincial offices. A new Taxpayer Education Call Centre provides an accessible, first point of contact for taxpayers and is staffed by eight people. The Taxpayer Advisory Unit, charged with leading taxpayer education efforts on the part of the ZRA, has a staff of five.

Box 29.1. **Objectives of taxpayer education in Zambia**

- Build excellent stakeholder relations, both internally and externally.
- Make revenue collection effective and efficient.
- Foster voluntary compliance.
- Educate taxpayers on their rights and obligations.
- Ensure that taxpayers understand tax laws and how to manage their tax obligations.
- Increase the number of citizens who pay taxes.
- Explain why taxes should be paid.
- Empower citizens to engage in discussions on the use of tax revenue.

Source: Zambia Revenue Authority.

The ZRA education programme is particularly aimed at personal income taxpayers (in both high and low tax brackets); corporate income taxpayers (including large-, medium-, small- and micro-size enterprises as well as state enterprises); youth; and the informal sector. The key activities are the dissemination of critical information such as taxpayers' rights and obligations, providing taxpayers with an understanding of these as well as the means by which to manage and fulfil them. As part of this, the ZRA has input into secondary and higher educational institutions, as well as community and/or cultural events. It also locates taxpayer services within other government offices to increase visibility and reach. It interacts directly with clients through seminars, lectures, training sessions, forums, workshops, briefings and dialogues. Use is also made of mass media (national, regional and local television, radio and newspapers), video programmes and printed materials such as guide books, pamphlets and public rulings, as well as various social media platforms (Facebook, Twitter, etc.).

In the first half of 2013 alone, the Taxpayer Education Unit carried out a television show on budget changes, workshops in colleges and universities as well as for business agencies, and weekly radio shows. A study tour to Nepal was conducted in May 2013, funded by the German Development Co-operation (GIZ) agency. This visit included five ZRA officials: the director and two officials from the Taxpayer Advisory Unit, one official from taxpayer services/domestic taxes and one official from taxpayer services/customs. The aim was to further feed into a taxpayer education strategy for Zambia.

Zambia has a consultative budgeting process in place between state and society, particularly geared towards non-state actors (Box 29.2).

Box 29.2. Zambia's tax consultative process between state and society

The government of Zambia, through the Ministry of Finance and National Planning (MoFNP), has put in place mechanisms through which non-state actors can submit tax and expenditure proposals to be considered in the national budget. This opportunity is increasingly being used by individuals, businesses, professional associations and civil society to lobby for tax concessions and exemptions, changes in tax administration and public expenditures, and to influence budget outcomes. In addition to lobbying through the formal budgetary process and structures, interest groups also use informal means to influence policy decision making.

Over the last decade, the government of Zambia and the private sector have initiated a more formalised consultative process through the Zambia Business Council (ZBC). This forum allows relevant government institutions and the private sector to discuss key policy issues. The objective is to generate ideas and dialogue with the government on institutional, regulatory and policy reforms to promote private sector development. The ZBC brings together four key Cabinet ministers (commerce trade and industry, finance and national planning, transport and communication, and agriculture) with the Zambia Development Agency, business associations and the Zambia International Advisory Council (comprised of well-established international business experts).

Source: adapted from Fjeldstad, O.-H. and K.K. Heggstad (2012), "Building taxpayer culture in Mozambique, Tanzania and Zambia: Achievements, challenges and policy recommendations", CMI Report, R 2012:1, Chr. Michelsen Institute, Bergen, available at: www.cmi.no/publications/publication/?4499=building-taxpayer-culture-in-mozambique.

In addition to working closely with Radio Phoenix (see below) and the television network, the ZRA has close relationships with the Ministry of Finance and National Planning and other government departments and agencies, schools, business organisations and GIZ.

Focus on: Tax chat on the radio

The ZRA reaches taxpayers through a weekly one-hour radio programme on Zambia's Radio Phoenix. This programme was initiated in March 2012 as a cheaper alternative to television for reaching a wide target group. The programme covers four out of the nine provinces in Zambia (Lusaka, Central and Copperbelt provinces, and part of the Southern province). In this way it reaches beyond the three provinces served by the ZRA.

The radio programme is aired live every Wednesday morning. The first half explains a tax matter – such as domestic tax, customs tax or changes in the administrative system – in the form of an interview between the Head of the ZRA Co-operation Communication Unit and a ZRA expert. The second half of the show involves a live call-in to allow taxpayers to ask questions, raise concerns or give feedback. The general public also provides feedback by email, face-to-face contact and by phoning the call centre. Criticism and feedback is used constructively to improve the show.

Initially, interviews for the radio programme were conducted by a station moderator. However, it was felt that the interviewer needed greater technical knowledge in order to pose relevant questions to the ZRA expert, so the Head or Deputy Head of the ZRA Co-operation Communication Unit now conducts the interviews.

This initiative is a team effort involving the entire Taxpayer Education Unit. The topics for each show are decided in a quarterly planning session run by the Taxpayer Education Unit. Topics may be proposed by staff or by listeners. ZRA officers from other divisions often have to be persuaded to participate in the programme as there is no formal requirement for them to participate in taxpayer education. The script for the show is drafted by an officer of the Taxpayer Education Unit every week and then reviewed within the team.

No specific training for this initiative has been given to the officers or anyone else participating in these interviews.

The annual contract with Radio Phoenix amounts to ZMW 47 000 (approximately USD 8 600). Currently there is no specific budget allocated for taxpayer education; the programme is entirely funded by the operational budget of the ZRA's Research and Planning Department.

Impacts

- Taxpayers reached. Radio Phoenix reaches four out of Zambia's nine provinces, covering an area of 643 km^2. The exact number of listeners is difficult to determine but the live call-in is very active and so the radio programme does increase taxpayers' knowledge.
- Perception changes. The programme has changed taxpayer perceptions of the ZRA. In the past people were rather uncomfortable about contact with the ZRA, but this seems to have changed due its new approach which sees citizens as partners (Box 29.3).
- Changes in tax compliance. Taxpayers are now more aware of their obligations and rights, which should increase compliance.

Box 29.3. Surveying taxpayer perceptions

In 2012, the Research and Planning Division conducted research into taxpayers' perceptions of the fairness and clarity of information provided by the ZRA. One question – answered by 79 taxpayers – asked them to state whether they knew that ZRA allows them: *i)* the right to appeal; *ii)* to pursue their rights and obligations; and *iii)* equitable treatment. If a taxpayer answered "yes" to all three questions, the perception is of fair treatment. The three aspects were weighted equally to compute a score for fairness.

This revealed that 73% of ZRA clients felt that they are treated fairly by ZRA staff. Similarly, out of a sample of 75 taxpayers, 96% stated that information on tax matters provided by the ZRA was clear.

Source: Zambia Revenue Authority (2012), *Taxpayer Charter Monitoring Report*, Second Quarter 2012, Research and Planning Division, Zambia Revenue Authority, Lusaka.

Lessons learnt

The fact that taxpayer education is not one of the core activities of ZRA officials who work in other departments means that there are limited incentives or time for them to participate. The Director of the Taxpayer Education Unit has attempted to resolve this by asking heads of divisions to lobby for staff participation within their divisions.

The radio programme is a new initiative and there has been no specific training for the moderators or presenters in public relations, presentational skills and handling queries in public. More could be done in this area.

Next steps

Currently there is no specific budget allocated for taxpayer education and so the operational budget of the ZRA's Research and Planning Department has been used to fund this initiative. Last year's taxpayer education activities were funded by the Public Expenditure Management and Financial Accountancy (PEMFA) under the Ministry of Finance. Resource constraints mean it will not be feasible to carry out all the taxpayer education activities planned for2013. These would have included shows on community radio stations all over Zambia; television adverts and programmes; workshops; inter-school debates on taxes; road shows and dramas; and brochures and leaflets.

Box 29.4. **Background on the Zambia Revenue Authority (ZRA)**

The ZRA was created in 1994 as a semi-autonomous agency under the Zambia Revenue Authority Act. Following Uganda's lead in 1992, Zambia became the second country in Africa to adopt the semi-autonomous model of a revenue authority. The ZRA has two operating divisions, the Domestic Taxes Division (Direct Taxes and VAT) and the Customs Services Division. Each of these divisions is headed by a commissioner. The ZRA's mission is to:

- be a world-class organisation recognised as a beacon of excellence in revenue administration
- optimise and sustain revenue collection through integrated, efficient, cost-effective and transparent systems, professionally managed to meet the expectations of all stakeholders
- assess, charge, levy and collect all revenue due to the government
- ensure that all revenue collected is credited to the Treasury.

For further information

- Website: www.zra.org.zm
- Facebook address: www.facebook.com/pages/Zambia-Revenue-Authority/456894244349519?fref=ts
- Taxpayer education e-mail address: advice@zra.org.zm

Source: Zambia Revenue Authority.

References

Fjeldstad, O.-H. and K.K. Heggstad (2012), "Building taxpayer culture in Mozambique, Tanzania and Zambia: Achievements, challenges and policy recommendations", CMI Report, R 2012:1, Chr. Michelsen Institute, Bergen, available at: www.cmi.no/publications/publication/?4499=building-taxpayer-culture-in-mozambique.

Zambia Revenue Authority (2012), *Taxpayer Charter Monitoring Report, Second Quarter 2012*, Research and Planning Division, Zambia Revenue Authority, Lusaka.

ORGANISATION FOR ECONOMIC CO-OPERATION AND DEVELOPMENT

The OECD is a unique forum where governments work together to address the economic, social and environmental challenges of globalisation. The OECD is also at the forefront of efforts to understand and to help governments respond to new developments and concerns, such as corporate governance, the information economy and the challenges of an ageing population. The Organisation provides a setting where governments can compare policy experiences, seek answers to common problems, identify good practice and work to co-ordinate domestic and international policies.

The OECD member countries are: Australia, Austria, Belgium, Canada, Chile, the Czech Republic, Denmark, Estonia, Finland, France, Germany, Greece, Hungary, Iceland, Ireland, Israel, Italy, Japan, Korea, Luxembourg, Mexico, the Netherlands, New Zealand, Norway, Poland, Portugal, the Slovak Republic, Slovenia, Spain, Sweden, Switzerland, Turkey, the United Kingdom and the United States. The European Commission takes part in the work of the OECD.

OECD Publishing disseminates widely the results of the Organisation's statistics gathering and research on economic, social and environmental issues, as well as the conventions, guidelines and standards agreed by its members.

THE INTERNATIONAL AND IBERO-AMERICAN FOUNDATION FOR ADMINISTRATION AND PUBLIC POLICIES (FIIAPP)

The International and Ibero-American Foundation for Administration and Public Policies (FIIAPP) is an international cooperation office of the Spanish government. Its objectives are to improve institutional and legal frameworks, the performance of government agencies and the quality of life of citizens in the countries where it operates. Primarily through public technical assistance (from the public sector to the public sector), it facilitates knowledge sharing and transfer, and mobilises over 1,100 civil servants each year to conduct studies and train senior officials and political leaders.

The Foundation is chaired by the Vice-President of the Spanish Government, and the heads of the Spanish Ministries of Foreign Affairs, Justice and Health serve on its board. Their presence, along with that of other important representatives of the Spanish government, guarantees the utmost institutional support for FIIAPP initiatives.

EUROSOCIAL II

Social cohesion is one of the key priorities in European Union (EU) and Latin America (LA) relations, as stated at successive summits in which the Heads of State and of Governments have agreed to back this bi-regional priority with resources and content by launching EUROsociAL. This is a European technical cooperation programme that reflects the growing concern over social cohesion, which is seen as a "common challenge" for the EU and LA.

EUROsociAL aims to consolidate a regional space for EU-LA policy dialogue around social cohesion. It is a horizontal and institutional programme that mobilises European and Latin American public expertise in a peer learning exercise. It uses a regional approach based on collaboration to address common challenges in the design, implementation, management and evaluation of policies intended to have a positive impact on social cohesion.

The grant for implementing EUROsociAL II (2011-2015) was awarded to a consortium, led by the International and Ibero-American Foundation for Administration and Public Policies (FIIAPP, Spain), which is made up of over 40 European and Latin American institutions.

OECD PUBLISHING, 2, rue André-Pascal, 75775 PARIS CEDEX 16
(23 2014 48 1 P) ISBN 978-92-64-22335-6 – 2015

www.ingramcontent.com/pod-product-compliance
Ingram Content Group UK Ltd.
Pitfield, Milton Keynes, MK11 3LW, UK
UKHW051501290926
15471UKWH00008B/1345

9 789264 223356